The SUNNI VANGUARD

THE SUNNI VANGUARD

Can Egypt, Turkey, and Saudi Arabia
Survive the New Middle East?

Jed Babbin   David P. Goldman   Herbert I. London

LONDONCENTER
FOR POLICY RESEARCH

The London Center for Policy Research
New York, New York
www.londoncenter.org

Designed by Kristina Phillips

ISBN 978-0615974477

Contents

Introduction

A SIX MONTH UNDERSTANDING between the P5+1 and Iran that includes the suspension of enriched uranium in return for the release of roughly seven billion dollars of Iranian assets frozen by the U.S. government, has set in motion a cascade of international events and issues. Foremost among them is the question of what should be done if Iran, based on this accord, can and will build nuclear weapons under the terms of the arrangement or in violation of it.

For nations such as Israel and Saudi Arabia this is an existential question. The Iranian government, on numerous occasions said that it would "wipe Israel from the map." Some argue that this is little more than rhetorical flourish but that conclusion is almost impossible to reach given the Iranians' pursuit of nuclear weapons. Israel is obliged to take Iran's statements with the utmost seriousness if Iran may soon have nuclear weapons and the missiles to deliver them, which is entirely possible.

It is also instructive that Saudi Arabian oil fields are located in the eastern part of the country in an area populated by Shia, despite the fact Saudi Arabia is a Sunni nation. An Iranian government with imperial ambitions to create a Shia Crescent has its eye on Saudi oil reserves.

One of the principal results emerging from the apparent U.S. rapprochement with Iran is a Sunni consolidation, what we have chosen to call a *Sunni Vanguard*. This group of nations is led by Egypt, the largest Arab and Sunni nation on the globe, Turkey, the most powerful military force in the Sunni world and Saudi Arabia, the richest of the Sunni nations. Each, in turn, has a reason to be suspicious of the U.S.-Iran accord and each in turn has reasons to be hostile to Iran.

The actions of these nations, independently and at times in concert, will have an enormous effect on the future of the Middle East. Therefore it is in the economic and national security interests of the United States to study these nations and, to the degree possible, forecast their stability which is, of course, the foundation of their ability to act.

The Egyptian military leadership harbors antipathy to those nations that supported the Muslim Brotherhood and the excesses of the Morsi government. Moreover, there is the belief Iranian Revolutionary Guard members insinuated themselves into the revolutionary street activism that ultimately toppled Mubarak and led to Morsi's ascendency. There is the additional fear that an Iran with nuclear weapons possesses a strategic advantage in any escalation scenario. Egypt's military assets compare favorably to Iran, but nuclear weapons alter the equation. In fact, Egypt has had deliberations with Saudi Arabia about "Sunni" nuclear weapons purchased from Pakistan and serving as a deterrent for both nations.

Turkey's foreign policy has been schizophrenic with both a commitment to NATO and overtures to NATO's enemies. However, the burdensome debt in Turkey undermining the economy is presently offset by Saudi bailouts. He who pays the bills often dictates the agenda. The Saudi princes exercise great leverage over Erdogan. Moreover, they (Turkey and Saudi Arabia) are on the same side supporting the rebels in Syria.

Saudi Arabia has had deep seated concerns about the Persians throughout its limited history as a nation. This isn't only Arab-Persian hostility, but Sunni-Shia distrust. Since Saudi Arabia now believes the United States is an unreliable ally, it has assumed the lead in organizing the major Sunni nations near Iran. Saudi influence is borne of wealth and a willingness to use "beneficence" to buy control. There is little doubt the Saudis can acquire nuclear weapons, and there have been conversations with Israeli leaders over a military option. Talk about history creating strange bedfellows.

What this means is that the Sunni Vanguard represents a tectonic shift in Middle Eastern affairs, arguably in world affairs. The leadership of Egypt, Turkey and Saudi Arabia may have their differences, but history has united them as a force. Iran's nuclear ambitions have created a

Sunni union that will exercise its military and financial strength for self-preservation.

For those who want to look over the horizon at the evolution of historical events, it is critical to examine the inner workings of the three important Sunni nations. This book is a start.

THE LONDON CENTER FOR POLICY RESEARCH STUDY CRITERIA

American foreign policy has always been more reactive than predictive. Most of the apparatuses of foreign policy have been like our foreign aid program, which has had little or no connection to policy objectives. Through alliances such as NATO, we have erected barriers to the effects of global events.

Despite those barriers, we have almost always been shocked by events over which we have no control. The Central Intelligence Agency and the State Department were just as surprised when the Berlin Wall was torn down in 1989 as they were when it was built in 1961. Even the stock markets, perhaps the best forecasters of global events ever devised, cannot do more than project trends. But there are, undeniably, events like that which should be predictable. Many analysts call these "black swan" events.

These events have three characteristics: first, they arrive unpredicted; second, they have an extraordinary impact, beyond what would be expected from them; and third, with the benefit of hindsight, people commonly label them as having been predictable.

This study is an effort to render such events more predictable.

These "gray swan events" are those which would otherwise be judged to be "black swan events" but for the fact that they are rendered predictable by our analysis. We do this not only by the application of logic to fact, but also to history. Cultures around the world are swept along by ideologies, religions, economic conditions—even the psychologies of nations—that make them more predictable than is generally accepted in government and academia.

The aim of this study is to determine how likely Egypt, Turkey and Saudi Arabia will be to suffer a major crisis within the next three to five years. We have developed five criteria under which we will analyze that nation in order to determine that likelihood. The criteria are:

1. Threats: The proximate causes of crises can properly be seen as threats to a nation's economic or physical security. Threats may be internal or external, regional or global, and because the kinds of crises we seek to forecast are not only those of armed conflict, we have to include threats to a nation's economy in any analysis. We shall consider issues such as demographics and possible resource exhaustion (oil, water, gas and more) to fully evaluate both the threats and the likelihood that they will, in the next three to five years, create a major crisis.

For many nations, especially those that seek to compete for power in the international arena—military power, economic power or both— the threat "matrices" can be highly complex and be comprised of a wide variety of threats. For the US, for example, we face threats from Chinese cyberwar, immigration, wealth transfer to the oil states, terrorism, the Iranian nuclear program and so many other threats of various severity that to make such an assessment will require a highly complex analysis even of how the threats may occur singly or in combination. For nations that do not compete on that level, such as Greece, their threat matrix may be purely a product of their own failed economy;

2. Alliances: Through history, military and economic alliances have served their members with uneven results. NATO, which grew out of the World War 2 Atlantic Alliance, seems to have shot its last bolt in Libya. SEATO never really functioned effectively. Economic alliances, such as the European Union, seem to function often more in form than in substance while OPEC, at times, has been highly effective. Alliances such as Iran's with Venezuela may provide a threat to freedom in this hemisphere. The UN, itself a supposed "alliance" among nations dedicated to peace, is certainly the greatest failure since the predecessor League of Nations. To properly judge threats to nations' economic or physical security we will garner sufficient facts to determine the functionality of a nation's alliances, the strength of those alliances and the terms of the alliances to judge whether and to what extent the allies will function to come to the aid of a crisis-beset member;

3. Investment in national security: To what degree is the nation investing in its own defense? Many of the EU's member nations have let us and NATO down by refusing to invest in their own defense. Other nations, such as China, face few and lesser threats but are investing very heavily in military assets designed to keep us out of their region. A subset of this factor is military preparedness: Israel is well prepared, but not for everything. In contrast, Italy has effectively abandoned preparedness. Italy, however, is a great deal more secure than Israel and many other states that exist in the shadow of existential threats. It can continue this course until its allies demand other conduct;

4. Ability to project power: Our diplomatic power is perceived to be waning but the U.S. still possesses greater military power projection capability than any other nation. Russia is pretending to have a great deal of such power and China is growing quickly in regional power projection ability though reluctant to admit it. Iran—through Hezbollah and directly with Iranian Revolutionary Guard Corps forces is projecting power as far as Syria and possibly as far as Central and South America. The ability to project power is, for nations such as Iran and Russia, an entirely negative influence on those regions within their reach. It is at least arguable that France's insistence on the intervention in Libya was out of greater concern for oil agreements than Libyan freedom and might be labeled neo-colonialist;

5. Strategic/economic security assessment: Russia eagerly seeks the status of international troublemaker or at least power broker. Oil and gas may pay for its ability to make that desire a reality. Spain and Italy are no threats to anyone due in part to the fact that they're in great financial distress. Pakistan may be the most dangerous nation in the world because of its nuclear arsenal, its claim to Kashmir and its Muslim ideology which may all combine to trump economic factors that might otherwise dissuade it from commencing a war. French demographics (as well as those of some other EU members) are very dangerous because of assimilation-resistant minorities which are mostly Muslim and which are a great drain on their economies. This factor may be regarded as the summary of the other four with one additional concept: time as an independent variable.

Time is an essential addition because it gives a context to the capabilities and intentions of other nations that intend—for good or for ill—to affect the studied nation's likelihood of suffering a crisis and its ability to deal with the crisis successfully.

* * *

Acknowledgments should be made to my two fellow authors, Jed Babbin and David Goldman, two of the nation's truly brilliant analysts and to those colleagues who helped erect the London Center for Policy Research.

TURKEY AT THE CROSSROADS

HERBERT I. LONDON

Introduction

WHY SHOULD ONE CARE about Turkey? Although it is a NATO member, geographically a bridge between Asia and Europe, its present leadership has tilted away from the United States. Our purpose is to project trends or, at the very least, to set a context for prediction in respect to Turkey because that nation played a key role throughout the Cold War and may—by its own or by the actions of others—soon be beset by crisis. The central question we address here is the likelihood of whether and how the government of Turkey may be rendered unstable in the next three to five years.

There are, in the analytical world, three kinds of events: relatively surprise-free events, moderately non-surprise free events and what some would call "black swan" events, which we sometimes modify to be "gray swan" events, "those rendered predictable by our analysis," but that are generally unpredictable. This booklet is an effort to assist with prediction, to make clear what seems ambiguous and to understand the nature of that ambiguity.

It would be foolhardy to offer a prediction 10 years into the future, but this analysis does contain three to five year scenarios organized around threats and threat levels, alliances and their role in creating a stable or unstable environment, national security concerns, the ability to project power, a strategic economic assessment and even a view of Turkey's cultural landscape that has some influence on the political environment.

Once the "sick man of Europe," and an empire disassembled after World War I, Turkey has emerged as a bridge between NATO and its western institutions and Islam, along with the religion's imperial ambitions.

Relying on Kemal Ataturk's secular orientation, Turkey was converted into a center of commercial activity after his election in 1924. Ataturk attempted to modernize Turkey by challenging strict Muslim traditions. In fact, western commentators employed Turkey as an example of how Islam could be moderated.

During the Cold War, Turkey became the military anchor for NATO's southern flank. Its army served with US and other allied forces in the Korean War in large part out of fear the Soviet Union would attempt to include Turkey in its orbit. Resources from the West poured into Turkey to buttress those military forces. At the moment Turkey has the second largest land force in NATO and the second largest air force. It recently acquired missile defense radars from China that are among the most sophisticated on the globe. For decades Turkey's military served as a bulwark against Islamic extremism.

Its armed forces consist of 890,000 personnel including 378,700 reserves. It has 4503 battle tanks, 310 reconnaissance vehicles, 650 armored infantry vehicles and 3643 armored personnel carriers, 7787 artillery pieces, more than 5813 mortars and 1363 attack missiles. In addition, it has two tactical air forces divided between east and west, including 338 combat capable aircraft (F5A/B, F-4E Phantoms and F-16 C/D) and a total of 1512 aircraft. The navy has 14 submarines, 18 frigates, 52 patrol boats and 27 mine countermeasure and warfare vessels. By any measure, even in a comparison with Iran's recently reinforced navy and land forces, Turkey is one of the most formidable military forces in the Middle East. Its military force is larger than Iran, Egypt and Saudi Arabia combined.

Since becoming prime minister in 2002, Recep Tayyip Erdogan has transformed his AKP party into a political movement that strives to oust and replace secular elites and traditional Turkish institutions that had bound the nation to Western values and American interests. The AKP was established as a reform to deal with the dismal state of the economy and Erdogan used his military authority to launch a political movement.

Prior to the rise of the AKP, Turkey was rooted in NATO, had a friendly relationship with Israel and could be relied on to tilt to the West on key foreign policy issues. That was yesteryear. Under Erdogan's leadership Turkey has emerged as a regional power claiming Ottoman imperial ambitions and, most notably, considers itself a leader in the Islamic world, particularly among Sunni Muslims. This sea change in attitude and policy has significant implications for the United States.

Some analysts in Washington still rely on a vision of Turkey as a bulwark against possible Russian aggression. Still others rely on Ataturk's modernization program, namely, economic growth as a decisive force against Erdogan's Islamization of Turkey. And then there are those who believe Turkey, despite the fear of Muslim emigration, can be a moderate addition to the European Union.

Erdogan apparently sees his nation's role differently. Based on his written and spoken commentary, the prime minister regards Turkey as *primus inter pares* among Muslim nations. Moreover, this desire for Muslim leadership has been accompanied with a distinctly anti-Western attitude. In part this attitude is understandable given Europe's rejection of Turkey as an EU member in 2001. But this policy shift goes beyond petty retaliation. He has noted that his dream is the restoration of the Ottoman caliphate.

On one matter, there isn't controversy: the United States has not resisted the Turkish strategic reorientation. President Obama is fond of saying Erdogan is his closest ally on the foreign stage. On almost any level this is an exaggeration, since Turkey may appear as an ally one day and an enemy the next. In fact, while President Obama still refers to Turkey as a Muslim "role model," this conciliatory viewpoint lacks both a sense of reality and a contingency plan to curtail the AKP's neo-Ottoman ambitions.

Time after time Erdogan has challenged essential U.S. interests. For example, Turkey continues to trade with Iran in violation of U.N.

sanctions. It is a sponsor of Hamas and engaged in, in fact promoted, the attempted break of the Israeli Gaza blockade. Most significantly, he hasn't been penalized for these actions by the U.S., in large part because the U.S. administration has not formulated a substantive strategy towards Turkey other than the apparently one-sided personal friendship between the two leaders. Despite assurances to the contrary, personal ties are not a policy.

Moreover, the prime minister has recently, 2013–2014, shown his repressive side by denouncing and arresting peaceful demonstrators as "provocateurs and terrorists." The conspiratorial theory is that an underground ultranationalist group called "Ergenokon" is bent on destabilizing the country, though evidence to support this claim is slim. Nonetheless, Erdogan's vindictive side is on display, giving even supporters reason for concern about his rule. Despite President Obama's often cited rationalizations, Erdogan is creating an environment in which his country's future will be determined by his whims. This internal policy is consistent with Erdogan's foreign policy.

In 2009 Erdogan transparently displayed his anti-Western stance by describing the imposition of sanctions against Iran's "peaceful" nuclear program as "arrogant." He even went so far as to contend that if the U.S. and Israel want Iran to give up its pursuit of nuclear weapons, they should be obliged to do the same.

But Erdogan is also a kind of political schizophrenic. Thus on the one hand, he does not envision Iran as an enemy; but on the other, he has allowed NATO to install an anti-missile radar facility on Turkish soil clearly designed to protect Europe from a potential Iranian missile threat. Some have argued this is a meaningless gesture designed to mollify his detractors in Europe and the U.S., and is not a transformative policy shift.

Turkey's goal appears to be evident based on most of its actions: a model oriented to Muslim supremacy with the immediate objective of binding Arab nations to a Turkish sphere of influence. At the very least, a hardheaded assessment of Turkey's strategic position is called for—with an emphasis on its regional ambitions and its internal schism between Islamic and secular forces.

Threats

The principal threats to Turkish stability (within the purview of this study) are (1) a military coup, which Erdogan is working to prevent by imprisoning generals; (2) spillover from the Syrian civil war, which Turkey is using its intelligence services to prevent but is otherwise vulnerable to; (3) a severe economic downturn that could neuter Erdogan's AKP; and (4) unrest in Kurdistan coming to a head in Turkey and fed by Iraq.

While Turkey has made a point of building a powerful military to counteract its dangerous neighbors, currently the chain of command is in disarray as a result of Erdogan's fear of a coup. With the resignation of Admiral Nusret Guner, the naval commander, in 2013 there are very few candidates to serve as his replacement.

As the *Economist* points out, more than half of Turkey's admirals are in jail, along with hundreds of generals and other officers accused of plotting against the Prime Minister. At last count one in five Turkish generals, including Ilker Basbug, a former chief of the general staff, was behind bars as part of the Ergenokon conspiracy. Others in an alleged coup plot, dubbed Sledgehammer, insist the evidence has been doctored (a claim reinforced by independent forensic experts) and have attempted to bring the matter to the U.N. Human Rights Council.

Prime Minister Erdogan has systematically reduced the generals' influence, but he is torn between the need for experienced commanders and the justifiable fear, based on historical precedent, that the commanders will engage in a coup. Since 1960 Turkey's army has overthrown at least four governments, with the bloodiest coup occurring in 1980 when 50 people were executed, 500,000 were arrested, and many hundreds died in jail. In 2007, the army tried to stop Abdullah Gul, a former foreign minister, from becoming Turkey's president. In 2008 the generals brought suit against the AKP in Constitutional Court for attempting to impose sharia law. The complaint was dismissed by a single vote. Yet even to this day millions of Turks, who fear a complete fundamentalist takeover of the country, revere the armed forces—albeit, recent well-publicized misdeeds such as scandal over corruption may be shifting opinion in another direction.

For Erdogan, the internal threat affects his perception of the external threat. As clashes with the Kurdish separatist PKK continue and the conflict in Syria threatens to spill over the border, Erdogan needs a defense force capable of dealing with these issues.

It may be an uneasy alliance, but Erdogan probably has the army under his control at the moment. The National Security Council that once imposed orders on civilian governments has been tethered. Army forces seemingly report to Erdogan through the chief of the general staff, Necdet Ozel, a fiercely loyal ally of the prime minister. Yet the generals remain a wild card subject to sway. The defense budget remains largely immune from civilian oversight. An internal service law that permits the army to intervene in politics remains in place.

Erdogan has learned his lesson well. In 1998 he said, "Democracy is just a train we board to reach our destination." In that year he was pushed off the train by the military and imprisoned for four months on the charge of "religious incitement" in the secular republic. When he returned to power in 2003 as prime minister, Erdogan exercised patience and prudence so as not to alarm military leaders. But after three successive elections in which the AKP party has increased its' plurality, he has been less bashful in promoting his program of creeping Islamization.

So clever was the strategy, and so eager were western allies to turn a blind eye toward Erdogan's radicalism, that they willingly acquiesced in his radical positions. In order to qualify, Turkey needed to place the military in a subordinate position to civilian authority. As a consequence, Erdogan subtly used European demands to defang the military, his potential rival, and the sole protector of secular democracy. In the past the Turkish military had a constitutional duty to preserve Ataturk's secular administration of the nation. But an emboldened Erdogan altered that constitutional provision in 2010.

The West's unwitting encouragement of Erdogan's Islamization program had the effect of de-democratizing the nation. This resulted in a foreign policy shift towards Sunni allies and open antagonism to Israel, a former ally. To demonstrate his position the prime minister was even willing to support the imprudent attempt by the Mavi Marmara to break the Gaza naval blockade, an Israeli effort to prevent the transfer of military material.

However, despite Erdogan's efforts Turkey remains an "official" secular state. In State Department missives this secular position is usually reaffirmed.

Whatever motives Erdogan displays at home are deeply affected by the instability in his neighborhood. In the Middle East nothing can be taken for granted. Long established alliances are shifting dramatically. As one political leader in the region noted, "The ground is shaking under our feet and we must keep all our options open." The election of Mohammed Morsi in Egypt in June 2012 and the subsequent coup against him in July 2013 raised and quickly lowered the impression of the Muslim Brotherhood as the heir apparent to Middle East leadership and a "force for stability."

The "old order," albeit not so old—before Mubarak's regime was overthrown in Egypt—had two axes: those of moderation and extremism. The axis of moderation—Egypt, Saudi Arabia, Jordan, UAE, and Kuwait— aligned with the West. It supported the Palestinian National Authority and encouraged a political settlement with Israel. The axis of resistance— Iran, Syria, Hamas, Hezbollah—has a strained relationship with the West and considers any settlement with Israel as surrender. Turkey maintains a foot in each camp—defending Iran, while also expressing public support for the Syrian rebels and refusing air rights for U.S. aircraft in Iraq.

However, the greatest miscalculation, in my judgment, lies in the Russian-U.S. agreement to destroy chemical weapons in Syria, an act which virtually assures the sustainability of the Assad regime. Turkey had hoped that the Assad government would be quickly eliminated with U.S. involvement, replaced by a regime aligned with the axis of moderation. To complicate matters further, President Obama and President Rouhani of Iran have been engaged in a melting of icy conditions on the nuclear weapons question. How this discussion will evolve is open to conjecture, but from Turkey's perspective it is yet another unpredictable dimension to the restructuring of regional alliances. If Erdogan's desire to be the regional power—a reassertion of Ottoman ambitions— is to be realized, he has an interest in putting an end to the bloodshed in

Syria and Iraq which is affecting Turkish stability and economic development. The emigration into Turkey form these wars has put an additional strain on the Turkish ecomony.

Recognizing the tension between the two axes, Turkey has engaged in back channel conversations with both. For example, there are reports that the Turkish foreign ministry has offered Iran information about various terrorists, including Abu Ghaith, the former spokesman for the al-Qaeda network, who was held by the police in Ankara and then released. Turkey also hardened its tone towards Egypt after the military ousted Morsi and his embattled loyalists. It recalled its ambassador to Cairo, encouraged pro-Morsi demonstrations across the country and cancelled joint naval exercises.

On the other hand, Erdogan employs sweet palliatives when talking about Turkey's role in establishing regional stability. Although talks with the Kurdish rebel PKK had been temporarily suspended, casting doubt on a peace process that could end a 30-year conflict, Erdogan holds out hope that a resolution will occur. He recently pointed out to President Obama that Turkey has absorbed 450,000 Syrian refugees. He has also been equivocal, one might even say mild, on the Obama administration's "detente" with Russia over the Syrian poison gas agreement, even though he eagerly wanted air strikes against the Assad government. It is noteworthy that the U.S. benefits from the use of its airbase in Incirlik Turkey, only 80 miles from Syrian territory.

As one might guess, there have been expressions of annoyance in the Turkish government over Obama's passivity and what some in Turkey have called his "betrayal." Prime Minister Erdogan's adviser, Yigit Bulut, said, "One hundred thousand people wouldn't have died in Syria if the U.S. had done what Erdogan said." He went on to note that "the world has a leadership problem. Today there are two and a half leaders in the world. One is Recep Tayyip Erdogan, the second is Putin and the other half is Obama."

On the other hand, Iran views Turkish support of the Syrian rebels as an attempt to weaken Tehran's influence over Assad and its Hezbollah surrogates. Erdogan might have recalled that Syria was the only Arab country that backed Iran during the eight-year long Iran-Iraq war, a move that solidified the strategic partnership between those two nations. Iran continually reminds Erdogan that as a member of NATO, a possible, albeit unlikely, member of the E.U., and a nation with bilateral ties to the U.S., distrust is part and parcel of the relationship. Hence Erdogan is encouraged to be a master juggler—or is it master poker player? My guess is the former, since Erdogan doesn't know when to "hold" and when to "fold." He often oversteps the boundaries of diplomatic arrangements leaving allies perplexed and enemies bemused.

Several threats to Erdogan's future and Turkey's stability should be noted: One is PKK attacks that lead to nationwide disruption. This is a low level threat that may warrant interest, but not concern. The Turkish military is strong enough to withstand any internal challenge. Two: a spillover of the war in Syria and the destabilization of Iraq. This is an issue since Turkey has absorbed more than 450,000 refugees from Syria, but this is a low-level border threat that is manageable. Three: a downturn in the economy that may result in a severe recession or inflationary spiral. This would be a major threat to Erdogan's future and his dream of uniting the offices of president and prime minister. It would also damage his party and lead to nationwide demonstrations. Four: a military coup to establish order that might ensue once mass demonstrations start that are not easily controlled by the government. The signs are already clear that Erdogan is concerned about such demonstrations and what they would mean for his political future. This—in my judgment—is the most serious threat, despite the seeming hold Erdogan has on the reins of authority.

Alliances

For Turkey there are several key alliances that purportedly reflect regional influence: The U.S. and Turkey; Turkey and its nearby neighbors; Turkey and NATO; Turkey and Muslim extremists.

At a 2013 face to face meeting with President Obama at the White House, Prime Minister Erdogan was accompanied by Hakan Fidan, Turkey's powerful spymaster and a man many consider the architect of Turkish regional security strategy. For many, Fidan is the face of the "new" Middle East, a barometer of Turkish foreign policy and regional development.

Fidan has been increasingly hostile to the U.S., especially its tentative and equivocal position after the Arab Spring. His rise in stature suggests an erosion in the U.S.–Turkish alliance. At the White House meeting, Fidan rejected the suggestion that Turkey's secret services have been aiding the radicals in North Africa.

However, there is evidence that Fidan passed sensitive intelligence data to Iran. In fact, several reports in 2013 indicate Turkey disclosed the identity of up to ten Iranians who were allegedly spying on Tehran for the Israeli Mossad. There was clear intent in this act: intimidate Israel. What is truly surprising is that Washington did not register a protest and the Obama government continues dealing with Fidan on sensitive matters. The decision to reveal the identity of the spies had to be approved by Erdogan, a point that makes the decision even more sinister than it may appear at first blush.

Despite ups and downs in Turkey's relationship with Israel, the Israeli spy agency had enjoyed a 50-year working relationship that is now imperiled.

The differences between the U.S. and Turkey on Syria are stark. Turkish officials believe an aggressive international effort on behalf of the rebels is the best way to remove Assad from power. The U.S. approach reflects a priority on ensuring that arms do not go to the jihadist groups, like al Qaeda, within Syria's rebel forces. For the U.S., the rebel groups may represent a bigger threat to U.S. interests than Assad, notwithstanding President Obama's passionate opposition to the use of poison gas.

What the Turkish position represents is a tilt in attitude, not a repudiation of the past. Erdogan surely realizes that any alliance with Iran is fragile. An imperial design on a Shia Crescent, the stated Iranian goal, cannot sit well with Erdogan's Sunni government. So too, Erdogan's desire to remove Assad and replace his hostile regime with one more favorable to Turkish interests is incompatible with Iran's goals. It is also notable that Erdogan wants to scuttle the prospect of a Kurdish state emerging from Syria's oil rich northeast.

Members of Syria's "moderate" opposition, to the extent it has a voice, noted that arms shipments were sent to the Muslim Brotherhood, the organization Erdogan's Islamist Justice and Development

Party has supported across the region, and even al Qaeda forces. President Obama's aides noted that "not all fighters are good fighters" and the Islamist extremists could harm the entire Middle East. When Erdogan is confronted with this evidence, he argues that Jabhat al Nusra, the anti-Assad rebels, could be dealt with later once Assad has been defeated.

In 2012 Turkey celebrated the 60th anniversary of its membership in NATO. NATO Secretary General Anders Fogh Rasmussen, accompanied by the Chairman of the Military Committee General Knud Bartels, visited Ankara and met with President Abdullah Gul and Minister of Foreign Affairs Ahmet Davcetoglu for the celebratory festivities. Turkey's "critical role" in shaping European security was emphasized. In fact, it was pointed out that Turkey doesn't just share European security, "it shapes it."

Ironically this may be more true than the Secretary General intended. When Turkey was first admitted into NATO, it was viewed as a bulwark against communist expansion in Europe's underbelly. Turkey was considered a key ally in the Cold War, a secular nation with democratic institutions and an economy about to take off. In 2013 Turkey undercut NATO security by holding war games with the Chinese Air force. NATO was never informed. Turkey also turned its back on the European Union and sought to join the Shanghai Cooperation Organization, a club for anti-Western dictatorships. The *coup de grace* was Turkish acceptance of a Chinese anti-aircraft system, which integrates a Chinese missile system into NATO's early warning network. What this means is that China will have access to top secret NATO software, which is tantamount to inviting the fox into the hen house. NATO does provide Turkey with security cover and protection, but it also offers Turkey leverage with potential enemies of the West.

Erdogan has made his foreign policy intentions clear by doing more than any other nation to help Iran skirt sanctions. Turkey's precious metals exports, almost all of which went directly or indirectly to Iran despite protestations from Washington, quintupled in 2012–13. In fact, the U.S. Senate measure to tighten sanctions on Iran, passed at the end of 2012, was aimed directly at Turkey's export of metals, including gold. Remarkably, Erdogan has asked NATO to station Patriot missiles on the Syrian border in order to help the rebels battle President Bashar al Assad, while at the same time cozying up to Iran and deploying a Chinese antimissile system. These contradictory acts led one wag to remark that Erdogan "is the geopolitical cognate of the Talented Mr. Ripley," Patricia Highsmith's fictional sociopath.

One might well ask, how does he get away with it? Although it enters the realm of speculation, I would guess every one of the countries that would call him to account, including the United States, worries that the region might be even worse off without him. Magician or sociopath? Take your pick. However, there is little doubt that Erdogan is not a reliable ally for the U.S. and perhaps not even for those neighbors he is now trying to embrace.

From an alliance standpoint, Erdogan demonstrates that Turkey as a model for alliance cohesion is a sham. He has been true to his word. He has embraced both Hamas and the genocidal Sudanese dictator Omar Bashir. He endorsed Yasim al-Qadi, a suspected al Qaeda financier. And, as noted, he has transformed Turkey into a sanctions busting lifeline for Iran. It would be reasonable to contend that Turkey, under present circumstances, doesn't belong in Europe, and it is probably dangerous to keep it within a consensus driven NATO.

Economic Assessment

Turkey has the 15th largest GDP in the world and the 17th largest nominal GDP. It is a founding member of the OECD and the G-20. During the first six decades of the republic, from 1923 to 1983, Turkey maintained a state dominated economy with strict government planning of the budget and orchestrated, but limited, private sector participation. In 1983 Prime Minister Turgut Ozal initiated modest market based reforms. These reforms, combined with foreign direct investments and loans, spurred rapid economic growth, punctuated by sharp recessions in 1994, 1999 (following the earthquake) and 2001.

The EU–Turkish Customs Union, which went into effect in January 1996, led to an extensive liberalization of tariff rates and a drop in public debt to GDP, from 75.9 percent in 2001 to 26.9 percent in 2013. An announced GDP growth of 6.8 percent annually from 2002 to 2007 made Turkey one of the fastest growing economies on the globe, although growth slowed to 1 percent in 2008 and in 2009 Turkey had negative growth during the worldwide recession of that period. Turkish GDP per capita adjusted, but purchasing power stands at about 52 percent of the EU average.

In 2010 the agricultural sector accounted for 9 percent of GDP, while the industrial sector accounted for 26 percent and the services sector 65 percent. However, agriculture accounts for 24 percent of employment. In 2004, it was estimated that 46 percent of total disposable income was concentrated in the top 20 percent of income earners, while the lowest 20 percent had 6 percent of the income, a disparity unchanged over the next decade. The rate of female employment is about 30 percent, the lowest among OECD nations.

These statistics, however, only reveal a very superficial understanding of the Turkish economy. In 2013, anti-government demonstrators and Turkish police engaged in violent street encounters over Erdogan's incipient Islamic dictatorship and his economic policies. While Turkey did enjoy a short-term economic boom from 2002 to 2007, it was promoted by a credit bubble that has left Turkish consumers in a belt-tightening mode and with a burdensome debt problem. Moody's AAA stamp on Turkish securities has quickly descended into the Baa category, which is still exaggerated. Should the economy remain in the doldrums, the anti-government demonstrators could be the advance guard for a regime change, a somewhat unlikely possibility at the moment, but not implausible.

Since Erdogan maintains national control through coercion and dispensing special favors, real economic power is in his AKP political party. It has made Erdogan a huge personal fortune and he has been generous to his loyalists. This accumulation of wealth in the hands of a small minority has not gone unnoticed. The Kurds, in particular, representing about one-fifth of the population with a fertility rate double that of Turkish natives, are a hostile minority concerned about rampant political corruption and jihadists supported by Erdogan.

Erdogan's mandate depends on economic performance. His Sunni fundamentalist agenda does not appeal to Turkey's majority (as a 2012

Pew Institute survey suggests). The AKP retains its power because of a widespread belief in Erdogan's ability to manage the economy effectively. This belief is illusory. The politically directed generosity of the government has come back to haunt consumers in the form of falling consumption rates, static GDP growth and an uptick in government spending. Most significantly, the formal economy workforce (i.e. salaried employment) declined by 5 percent in 2013.

In order to sustain the consumer bubble, Turkey reached a current account deficit of 10 percent in 2012, financed by short-term debt instruments of Sunni Gulf states. Turkey's short-term foreign debt is still growing at 30 percent annually and more than twice as high through 2013. Consumer debt outstanding has risen tenfold since 2006 and jumped by 40 percent in 2012, a condition marked by consumer borrowing to refinance the interest on existing debt. Erdogan's spending spree has left Turkey with an enormous debt burden. This is comparable to consuming alcohol that can be exhilarating, but the resulting hangover quite unpleasant. That is the emerging Turkish economic story. Banks cannot book loans at 40 percent a year indefinitely and consumers cannot keep borrowing to maintain a lifestyle to which they have become accustomed. In retrospect, Erdogan's Islamism may be a belated attempt to heal the fissures in the economy through religious adherence. In a country that knew secularism for much of the twentieth century, Erdogan's strategy will probably not work.

As David Goldman points out in a 2011 *Asia Times* article, "A developing country cannot sustain a fertility rate that leads to a rapid increase in elderly dependents, yet the fertility rate of Turks for whom Turkish is a first language has been in steady decline over the past fifteen years, falling to only 1.5—equal to that of Europe—while its population is aging almost as fast as Iran's, leaving the country's social security system with a deficit of close to 5 percent of GDP." Even Erdogan noted, "If we continue the existing [fertility] trend, 2038 will mark disaster for us." That disaster is creeping up inexorably.

Despite this rather dismal picture, it is appropriate to ask how Turkey has managed to persuade many nations across the globe that it is an economic success.

Although it is not a part of official statistics, Turkey's gold shipments to Iran, in violation of U.N. restrictions, are enough to make a major dent in the country's current account deficit. At an annual rate of about $18 billion, Turkish gold exports amount to 2.2 percent of gross domestic product. Without these exports Turkey's bulging trade deficit would explode. While the external debt is relatively low (but growing rapidly), two thirds of the short-term debt is owned by banks, and the evidence suggests that most interbank money comes from Saudi Arabia and other Gulf states. If the Saudis, for example, decline to roll over Turkish bank obligations, the nation would be paralyzed in weeks.

Moreover, the Saudis have good reason to distrust Erdogan. After all, he has developed close ties to Iran; he is promoting the Muslim Brotherhood in Syria and elsewhere; and he often talks as if he is the leader of the Sunni world. However, the Saudis also realize that Turkey's impressive military force represents the only real counter-weight in the region to Iranian ambitions. The interbank money Saudi Arabia provides for Turkey might be considered an insurance policy, but if the Saudis become impatient, they could pull the plug on Turkey's economy.

It is equally ironic that Russia, which has leverage over Turkey as its main supplier of natural gas, finds itself opposing the Turkish position in Syria. While this difference is a source of tension, the Russians have good reason to hope for Turkey's stability. With millions of Muslims in the Caucasus, the Russians are eager to have Turkish forces protect their southern border.

With President Putin outfoxing President Obama in his protection of Syrian President Assad from U.S. attack and with the Morsi government overthrown by a military coup, the Erdogan stance in Syria and his approval of the Muslim Brotherhood look ill advised. Erdogan now equivocates on regional matters as this volatile situation evolves, constantly looking over his shoulder at Russian and Saudi strategic decisions. He had better do so if he wants Russian energy sources and Saudi money.

Nevertheless, the debt bomb is real and ticking. Economic growth is a distant memory. Turkish banks, in order to reduce their foreign dependency, lend their customers just enough to pay the interest on past loans. Many Turks are caught in a consumer debt spiral, borrowing to pay a 32 percent interest rate on credit card obligations. That is clearly unsustainable. The question is if and when the Turkish people will express their anger at Erdogan and his government. The debt bomb is a threat, not only for Turkey's economy, but for Erdogan as Turkey's leader.

In a period of four months, Turkey's investment-grade credit rating went from an all-time high to an astonishing slide. The benchmark Istanbul stock index lost one third of its value since reaching its apogee in 2008. The Turkish lira has plummeted to record lows and bond yields have doubled to ten percent. Despite the effort of Turkey's Central Bank to stem the declines through the spending of 15 percent of its net reserves, the decline continues. This downturn has undermined the government's claim to have transformed the traditional boom and bust economy and is threatening Erdogan's bid to extend his 10-year rule.

The days when Turkey was considered a market darling are over, as almost every economist in Turkey has noted. What remains is either crisis or slow growth that will seem like a recession. The contrast with the recent past is stark. In nominal terms, gross domestic product expanded by an average of 5 percent annually since the Justice and Development party or AKP came to power in 2003. Per capita income tripled to more than $13,000, yielding three successive election victories for Erdogan.

In 2011 the bumpy ride began with credit-fueled consumer spending and the current account deficit ballooning to a record $78.4 billion or 10 percent of GDP. Fears about Turkey's ability to repay short term foreign debt caused a run on the lira that lost 20 percent against the dollar. The drop triggered double-digit inflation and a slowdown in growth of more than 6.5 percent. An economy dependent on imports and foreign capital magnified the losses and the slowdown. The International Monetary Fund warned that "were global liquidity to dry up or risk appetite turn sour, the economy [Turkish] would be forced into a sharp adjustment."

Metro Poll, one of Turkey's leading pollsters, said that 2013 support for the ruling party slipped to 43 percent from a peak of 52 percent in 2011. Recognizing this downturn in popularity, Erdogan in September 2013 announced a reform package to bolster his political standing. This cocktail of legislative and administrative reforms includes a provision under which the state will return land belonging to Mor Gabriel, the world's oldest Syriac monastery and one that represents a non-Turkish domination within Turkey, that had not received recognition in the past.

Most significantly, Erdogan reached out to the Kurds, the country's largest ethnic minority, even conceding that pupils in state run schools no longer have to declare every Monday, "I am a Turk," a provision introduced in 2002. Although the reforms do not satisfy most Kurds, they have lifted the gloom that beset the country after the government's brutal response to mass protests in June 2013, which claimed five lives and was widely regarded as a "human rights violation on a huge scale." Erdogan was also the first Turkish leader to publicize peace talks with Abdullah Ocalan, the imprisoned leader of the rebel Kurdistan Workers' Party (PKK). For the moment, at least, Erdogan has neutralized Kurdish anti-government sentiment which, if joined with economic protests, would lead ultimately to a wave of nationwide unrest. These reform measures are not merely an exercise in liberalization, but rather a distraction from the coming economic downturn.

Strategic/Economic Security Assessment

As Turkey's ruling AKP party considers its 100th anniversary in 2023, there is much exaggerated rhetoric about Turkey aiming to become one of the world's ten largest economies, with a target per capita GDP of $25,000 (inflation adjusted). With current per capita GDP presently at about half that dollar figure the scale of ambition is considerable. Growth, which is the only way to meet this ambitious goal, will be the vital element underpinning the government's strategy in the years to come, but that growth is dependent on inexpensive energy and electricity. At the moment Turkey imports 92 percent of its oil and 98 percent of its natural gas. More than half of the oil comes from Iran and 55 percent of the gas from Russia.

Turkey's dependency on energy imports for sustainable growth negatively affects its current account balance and Turkey's macroeconomic stability. With the likelihood of an increase in sovereign debt to investment, a current account deficit is an issue the government must overcome. Linked to this problem is the increased demand for electricity and possible supply shortages if demand increases at the current and projected rates of seven or eight percent a year. To address this issue Ankara is developing renewable and nuclear facilities, but these innovations have a significant time horizon. In the short term, this translates into a reliance on imported hydrocarbons, i.e. Iranian oil and Russian gas.

In an effort to avoid dependency on two nations, Turkish emissaries have visited Iraq's Kurdish region and have cultivated a relationship with Kurdistan Prime Minister Barzani. At play is a pipeline between northern Iraq and Ceyhan, Turkey which has the potential of one million barrels a day, enough to meet current Turkish needs. The first pipeline should be completed by the end of 2013 and the second in 2014. However, Baghdad has balked at this development, claiming the Kurdish region cannot negotiate the terms unilaterally.

While the economic case is compelling, the politics are far more complicated. Turkish domestic political dynamics are volatile, Iraq's even more so. For example, how the Turkish government and the Kurdistan Workers' Party (PKK) interact could affect Ankara's ability to guarantee the safe passage of energy sources through its south-east territory. Foreign entities obviously play key roles as well. If the Iraqi federal government attempts to prevent the Kurdish oil pipelines from completion, Turkey may be put in a very uncomfortable position. Similarly, the Russians could turn off the gas spigot at any time, particularly when Turkish political judgment isn't consistent with Putin's foreign policy perspective. This fear is even more pronounced with Iran, which explains why Turkey has not been outspokenly opposed to Iran's rush to enrich uranium and develop nuclear weapons. In a sign that Turkey's policy makers are keen on reducing Russian gas imports, the government said in December 2012 that it would not take part in Russian's South Stream pipeline project. But finding alternatives has been complicated. Keep in mind Turkey is likely to overtake Britain as Europe's third biggest electricity consumer before 2020. It is scrambling to meet energy demands and simultaneously to assuage nations on which it relies.

Turkish Energy and Natural Resources Minister Taner Yildiz plans to have Turkey purchase one million tons of crude oil from Libya in an effort to reduce reliance on Iranian oil. Not only does this purchase serve Turkey's energy needs, but it has led to a waiver from sanctions the United States imposed on countries buying oil from Iran. Although this policy makes sense, it could lead to retaliation from Iran since Iran has influence in and ties to the PKK, often referred to as a terrorist organization. Proximity and existing transport systems have encouraged reliance on Libya and Iran rather than allies in the Sunni world.

Turkey's energy needs, economic policy and foreign affairs are linked in a tightly wound nest of thorns. For economic growth to occur, energy requirements must be met. For energy requirements to be met Turkey must engage its neighbors and Sunni Gulf states in an artful minuet in which partners change, but no one is left rejected.

Ability to Project Power

Turkey is without question the most formidable military force in the Middle East, if one excludes Russia and the United States from the equation. Its land and air forces are, as already noted, the second largest in NATO. Turkey also has what is arguably the most sophisticated anti-missile system in the region provided by the Chinese through "stolen" Raytheon technology.

Its ties to NATO provide additional technical and logistical support, albeit sensitive data including software programs and battle plans are available to enemies of NATO as well. China's military largesse comes with a price tag. Similarly, Turkey's reliance on Iranian oil could lead to a compromise in security arrangements with the West.

As of this report, Turkey does not have a military rival even though it does have a presumptive enemy, Israel. But like everything in the Middle East, the relationship with Israel is complex. For decades, Turkey and Israel maintained close commercial ties. Even now, back channel communication between the two nations is ongoing. When Erdogan encouraged Islamization, the Palestinian issue rose in importance at the same time. Public condemnation of Israel became commonplace in Turkey's political circles. The military was purged of any pro-Israeli or even neutral factions. Whether this sentiment remains intact in a post-Erdogan era is problematic, since commercial interests in Turkey are eager to resume ties to Israel.

Turkey's F-16's certainly have the range to reach Israel, but any adventurous effort other than sending a ship load of volunteers to break the economic blockade against Gaza is unlikely. In fact, even another *Mavi Marmara* effort is unlikely. Turkey understands Israel's military strength and ability to retaliate, notwithstanding its recently deployed anti-missile system and advanced radars.

The big strategic question involves Iran. Despite the present cozy relationship, tensions between the two states could mount easily. A nuclear-armed Iran intent on pursuing its imperial ambitions to create a "Shia crescent" would lead inevitably to a hostile response. For Turkish strategic analysts, the issue in any prospective escalation scenario is how to neutralize Iran's nuclear capability. Preemption might be an option, but one fraught with tactical complications. The only *unlikely* scenario is an imperial Iran using its nuclear advantage attempting to forcibly insinuate itself into Turkish society. This is a do or die proposition that enters the realm of extreme speculation, since Turkey's conventional forces are far superior to Iran's.

Moreover, Erdogan has employed a fantasy of his own dealing with the reclamation of the Ottoman Empire. Sunni nations in the Gulf may admire Erdogan's bravado; but they certainly would mind Turkish muscle flexing. It is not surprising that Turkey has aligned itself with the rebels in Syria. The civil war has emerged, to some degree, as a Sunni-Shia struggle. When these religious factions have a common enemy, e.g. Israel, they unite. But in the absence of a commonly held foe, they divide. That division might well suggest historical evolution in the region.

National Character

Since Ataturk, Turkey has moved inexorably toward a secular state increasingly westernized with commercial interests across the globe. While there has been a cultural schism between west and east Turkey and between rural and urban areas, a shift towards modernization or westernization evolved over an eight decade period. When extremist sentiments popped up during this era, they were crushed by military officers who represented the secular mindset.

When Erdogan was elected in 2002, conditions gradually started to change—or so it seemed. Islam was exalted as both a religion and a national cultural force. While most polls indicate the Turkish people did not fully embrace this ideological orientation, many did. However, Erdogan's electoral success was due more to the extraordinary success of his economic policy than his Islamization program. After purging the military of unsympathetic officers, Erdogan felt secure in pursuing his religious goals. He moved gradually but relentlessly until his hold on political authority seemed unchallengeable. He treated his enemies brutally and his friends with tender loving care. It seemed to work until the downturn in the world economy and the credit crunch in 2008. Erdogan, as was the case with many leaders, attempted to stimulate the economy by floating debt. The strategy had a salutary effect by offering credit at reasonable rates to prospective borrowers. But by 2011, the debt burden on the national treasury and on individual borrowers reached devastating levels. At this point, bank loans were restricted in order to tighten credit; the net effect was that borrowers could only obtain loans up to the level of interest payments, as was already noted. Belt tightening has become a national concern and the once invincible Mr. Erdogan has been placed in a very dicey political position. Despite a firm hold on the military and a crackdown on protestors, he is no longer a widely admired figure.

Recent polls indicate he has lost majority support across the country. Of course, as a man with few scruples, he could manipulate the next election by demonizing or even eliminating his political rivals. The most interesting development is that in the recent past Erdogan could adapt his Islamic program without much opposition because of the relative strength of the economy. With the economic downturn, that is no longer the case. Now there is active debate and dispute over Islam's role in the future of Turkey. What has resurfaced is the Ataturk world view that suffused the culture for eighty years and continues to hold a tight grip on a majority of the people. How this wrestling match between the Islamic view and secularization will turn out hinges on Erdogan's ability of to improve economic conditions.

Conclusions

In many ways Turkey is a bridge between both Asia and Europe and between Islam and modernity. The Chinese government, which has developed a keen interest in Turkey, and has invested heavily there in the last few years, recognizes the geostrategic importance of this nation. Lying between Russia and the Middle East, Turkey is a tempting ally for China.

The United States realizes the importance of Turkey as well. It is a key NATO member and a gateway to Iran diplomatically. For western nations, it is imperative to keep Turkey within the axis of moderation, even as Erdogan enhances his political leverage by appearing as a moderate one day and an extremist the next.

U.S. analysts should also note that Erdogan's political position is far more fragile than they often assume. The "magician of the Turkish economic miracle" has been transformed into "a bungler" with extreme religious views. While Turkey has assumed the leadership of Sunni nations, the Shia-Sunni schism over Syria poses long term issues for the region. An Iran with nuclear weapons would most likely trigger proliferation in Sunni nations and a world far more dangerous than it is at the moment.

If Turkey is ousted from NATO—an admittedly unlikely event— because it is regarded as an unreliable ally, it could use its powerful military force to promote its own imperial interests.

In many respects Turkey is a schizophrenic's dream. It is a nation divided by geography, politics and ideology. It is both moderate and extreme. It wants to enter the 21st century and simultaneously return to the 7th century. It is pro-West and anti-West. It is with the United States and against it. It is an economic miracle and a debt riddled nation. It is "sick" and "well." In fact, at any given time almost anything one says about Turkey could be true.

Despite these internal contradictions, there is sufficient empirical basis for predictions. The PKK, for example, while a threat to oil pipelines and fomenting urban violence, is not a major threat to Erdogan's tenure. For that matter, Erdogan's foreign policy—which has simultaneously irritated Saudi Arabia, the United States to some degree, Iran, and Iraq—poses a minimal influence on Turkey's immediate future.

What will make a difference is the state of the economy. The debt burden, including personal debt, will not only serve as a severe drag on the economy, it could drive a deep recession putting Erdogan's political future in jeopardy. The other wild card is the Saudi assumption of Turkish debt and the appetite of the Saudi family to continue this arrangement.

I believe the Gulf States have too great an investment in Turkey's stability to let it fail. As noted, no one may trust Erdogan, but it is better to rely on the devil you know.

The Obama administration's adoption of the Russian plan for Syria, thereby reinforcing Assad's position, and the apparent rapprochement with Iran over nuclear weapons have caused immense turmoil in Turkish strategy. It is not clear whether Erdogan should tilt further to Iran or enhance his position with the United States. As I see it, Erdogan is increasingly inclined to try to keep a footprint in each camp, a strategy that in the long run is not sustainable. In the short term, however, it may work because U.S. policy is unclear and a deal over nuclear weapons with Iran may yet be ironed out.

Turkey's role as a regional influence has diminished and will continue to diminish with the accession of the military government in Egypt. Turkey played its Morsi and Muslim Brotherhood hand and lost. That hand was not only a losing one on the foreign stage, but likely to be a losing one at home. Despite gradual successes and Erdogan's coercive measures, Turkey is not ready for an Islamic set of laws and conditions. In fact, should Erdogan continue to pursue this path as vigorously as he has, it will be his undoing.

If there is a "gray swan" in this scenario that could destabilize Turkey it is an unanticipated electoral defeat for Erdogan followed by a military junta—notwithstanding the purging of military officers—that establishes order after a spasm of nationwide violence due to the sputtering economy. As I see it, this is the most likely roadmap to the future of Turkey.

Like all forecasts, of course, this one is risky since there are always a host of imponderables this study did not consider. But we at the London Center for Policy Research believe that this kind of futurist analysis is imperative in order to plan for policy responses in the three to five years to follow.

At the end of 2013 and the beginning of 2014 the dreams of Recep Tayyip Erdogan, Prime Minister of Turkey, seem to be evaporating under the Istanbul sky. His party The Justice and Development party (AKP), is in disarray; a major corruption and bribery scandal has led to accusations about cabinet members and their families. The investigation prompted Erdogan to say "The judiciary will pay."

With an election in March, Erdogan's monolithic hold on the nation seems tenuous. The rifts, glossed over after three successive electoral victories, have reemerged. Mr. Erdogan's attacks on police officials, prosecutors and members of his cabinet have revealed the internal fracturing.

One of the cabinet ministers who lost his job in the aftermath of the corruption revelations refused to go quietly; instead calling for Erdogan's resignation. Departing lawmakers criticized the government for blocking the graft probe, which Erdogan has described as an international smear campaign. At this stage, it is difficult to know if Erdogan can withstand the pressure. But if he does, Turkey will either be under strict authoritarian rule or helplessly afloat politically.

The political turmoil is reverberating on the streets with thousands of protestors marching against the government in Ankara, Izmir and Istanbul. Most significantly, the economy, once described as the miracle in the Middle East, has been faltering since 2008. The lira has plummeted more than seven percent against the dollar and euro since mid-December. Erdogan's government borrowing costs hit 10.37 percent, the highest in two years while the stock market slumped 15 percent.

The fragility of the Turkish economy has been evident for several years with a behemoth debt burden serving as an albatross on the economy. Personal borrowing has been restricted by banks suggesting that the financial structure cannot sustain the political risk now confronting the nation. Confidence in Turkey's financial system is at its lowest point in 25 years.

Since foreign direct investment has been a key factor in "the decade of prosperity" (2002-2008), financial interests may be looking in a different direction. As has been noted, in recent years Saudi Arabia has invested heavily in Turkey for both financial, political and religious reasons. With political uncertainty of the moment, that financial spigot could be turned off forcing the Turkish economy into a deep recession.

The regional implications for these events is profound. Turkey is a member of NATO and some would contend remains in the Middle East Axis of Moderation, albeit hardly a reliable member of this group. It has a secular tradition going back to the era of Ataturk, but Erdogan has attempted to Islamicize the state along Sunni lines. From a balance of power perspective, Turkey could serve as a counter-weight to Iranian ambitions with its powerful military force, a fact that is very much in the forefront of Saudi strategic considerations.

Although President Obama has called Prime Minister Erdogan "his closest ally," relations have grown frosty over the U.S. rapprochment with Iran and the unwillingness of America to assist the rebels in Syria. Nonetheless, Turkey, through NATO, does represent U.S. interests in the region. A Turkey in disarray is not desirable from the State Department point of view.

Erdogan may have purged the military of potential opponents, but the historical antecedents remain very much in the mind of the Turkish people. A military coup to maintain order is a possibility should the level of instability worsen. This condition has not only happened several times in the recent past, it is Turkey's way of dealing with disorder.

SAUDI ARABIA'S PRECARIOUS BALANCE

JED BABBIN

Introduction

SAUDI ARABIA, THE WORLD'S principal source of fossil fuels, is the face Islam presents to the West. Its preeminence in the sale of oil and gas and its moderate image led to a bow by the president of the United States to the Saudi king in May 2009.

Saudi Arabia contains the two holiest sites in Islam—Mecca and Medina—so important an element of the nation's prestige that it is part of its king's title: "custodian of the two holy mosques." And its place atop the world's economy seems secure, threatened only by the impossible and the improbable.

Saudi Arabia appears to be a stable monolith. Its royal family—which has as many as 24,000 members—is careful to cultivate a "different yet the same" image in the eyes of the western policymakers and media.

But Saudi Arabia is more a study in conflicts than a stable monolith. The gerontocracy of its royal family rules in conjunction with a heavy-handed theocratic council that allows no religious freedom or any of the other freedoms that Americans take for granted. And that partnership rules a nation that is of an average age of less than 25. Though its elites are extremely wealthy, the unemployment rate is over ten percent. It oppresses many of the foreigners who come there to work.

If there is a danger that the Saudi royal family's government could fall, it would be in the economic and national security interests of the United States and several other nations to reduce the severity of it or prevent that danger from arising. The purpose of this study is to help policymakers determine whether and when such dangers may arise, looking forward for only a short period, the next three to five years.

It would be easy—and wrong—to conclude that Saudi Arabia will remain stable as long as oil prices remain high. It would be just as easy—and just as wrong—to predict that its population will revolt against its theocracy in some revival of the "Arab Spring."

Why Saudi Arabia was largely unaffected by the "Arab Spring" is worthy of considered study, as is the question of the nation's stability in the short and long term. Any analytical tool that can help policymakers judge the stability—and, therefore, the risks—attendant to economic, diplomatic and military transactions with the nation can be a substantial assistance to the formation of policy in each of those spheres.

Saudi Arabia's Political-Religious Economy

Saudi Arabia's society—including its economy—was created by two factors: oil and religion.

The Kingdom possesses about 17% of the world's proven oil reserves.[1] Of its Gross Domestic Product—which was about $927.1 billion in 2012—about 80% of budget revenue and 90% of export earnings come from petroleum sales.[2]

The US Energy Information Administration estimates that Saudi Arabia exports approximately 11.7 million barrels of oil per day.[3] Its capacity to refine oil for export and domestic consumption is about 18% of production capacity.[4] (More than fifty percent of Saudi Arabia's oil went to the Far East in 2012.[5])

With a population of almost 27 million, Saudi's labor force is only about 8 million and its unemployment rate is a relatively high 10.6%.[6]

---

[1] CIA World Factbook, www.cia.gov

[2] Id.

[3] USIA Country Brief, http://www.eia.gov/

[4] Id.

[5] Id.

[6] CIA World Factbook, supra

Of those unemployed, some 34% are women, 86% of those receiving unemployment benefits are women and 40% of those women are college educated.[7]

Those figures are somewhat misleading. Of the 8 million in the labor force, about 80% of those people are citizens of foreign nations.[8] That means only about 1.6 million Saudis are part of the labor force, and a substantial number of them are employees of the government.

Just how many are government employees is not entirely clear. In 2001, the Saudi Central Department of Statistics estimated that 3 million Saudis were employed in the country and unofficial estimates were considerably higher.[9] If we do the math, the numbers don't work out. There can't be only 1.6 million Saudis as part of the labor force if perhaps 3 million are employed by the government (unless you do not count government jobs as employment). There is a substantial number of Saudis employed by foreign companies as a result of aggressive "Saudization" programs since 2011.

But the numbers—whatever they are—must work at some point, as do the reasons for them. The most important numbers are not those which describe the work force but those that describe oil exports. If 80% of GDP and 90% of export earnings are attributable solely to petroleum exports the most important conclusion the facts allow is that Saudi Arabia is what economists call a "rentier" state.

More precisely Saudi Arabia is a Wahabbist-rentier state. Its income is derived from "rents"—i.e., the export of petroleum and petroleum products—and not from productive work. Arguably, at least, Saudi Arabia was a rentier state even before the oil booms of the previous century. The royal family had, since the nation was founded, been able to obtain "rents"—i.e., fees and taxes—from Muslim pilgrims to Mecca and Medina as well as other tariffs and fees.[10] As one analyst explains, "At its most basic assumption, [rentier state theory] holds that, since the state receives its external income and distributes it to society, it is relieved of having to impose taxation, which in turn means that it does not have to

---

[7] Washington Post, Nov. 13, 2012

[8] CIA World Factbook, supra.

[9] Hertog, "Princes, Brokers and Bureaucrats," Cornell University Press (2010), p. 187.

[10] Id.

offer concessions to society such as a democratic bargain or a development strategy."[11]Wahhabism Dominates Saudi Arabia's Societal Functions
Where many experts and analysts go wrong, however, is in calculating
how independent from internal religious-ideological considerations the
Saudi-rentiers have been and can be.

Matthew Gray cites what he calls "conditional rentierism." He wrote,
"A common example is Saudi Arabia, where the state arguably has enjoyed
a comparative amount of freedom from specific interest groups in pro-
ceeding with its economic and development policies, it still has done so
in the interests of state-building and to reinforce its legitimacy."

Gray's formulation is only partially correct. While the Saudi state
may have enjoyed a comparative amount of freedom from special interest groups—compared to other Muslim states in the Gulf region—it is
entirely captive of one: the Wahabbi sect of Islam.

What "Wahhabism" Means in Saudi Arabia

Before it became Saudi Arabia, the land was called "Nejed." And after
T.E. Lawrence's campaign with Arab forces against the Turks in World
War I, there was John Bagot Glubb.

Egyptian Hassan al-Banna (1906-1949) is credited with the creation
in 1928 of the Muslim Brotherhood—the "Ikhwan" - a fundamentalist
Islamic organization. The Brotherhood is a radical Islamic organization
that from its inception based its creed on global jihad and views terrorism as a legitimate tool of policy.[12] But another "Ikhwan"—another even
more violent "Brotherhood"—was born in "the Nejed" before al-Banna's group appeared.

Glubb, like Lawrence, rose to great notoriety. Eventually he was
knighted and elevated to the rank of lieutenant-general and led an Arab
force against the Israelis in the Israeli War of Independence.

According to Glubb, the Nejed's sultan in 1912, Abdul Aziz ibn Saud,
sponsored a revival of Wahhabism.[13] The revival came after almost an

---

[11] Gray, "A Theory of Late Rentierism in the Arab States of the Gulf," http://www12.
georgetown.edu/sfs/qatar/cirs/MatthewGrayOccasionalPaper.pdf

[12] Lopez, "History of Muslim Brotherhood Penetration of the US Government," April
2013, (http://www.gatestoneinstitute.org/3672/muslim-brotherhood-us-government).

[13] "War in the Desert," supra, p. 58.

entire century of warfare that eventually suppressed the Wahhabis. The Wahhabis moved to new settlements in Nejed and assumed the title of "Al Ikhwan,"the brethren.[14]In July 1920, John Bagot Glubb was posted to Iraq as a junior army officer loaned to the RAF. His assignment was to protect nomadic tribes in southern Iraq from raiding bands of Ikhwan. The raiders would roam into Iraq, seeking to kill Muslims who weren't Wahhabis and pillage their settlements. Equipped with only a few aged aircraft and armored cars, Glubb found his mission almost impossible. By March 1, 1924, Glubb had still not been able to establish any sort of defense from the persistent Ikhwan raids.[15]Like Lawrence, Glubb was an "Arabist." At the height of his career, he led the Trans-Jordan's "Arab Legion" against Israeli forces in Israel's war of independence in 1947-48. In every sense, he was sympathetic to Arabs. But not to Wahhabis. As he wrote later,

> *From the point of view of the Muslim religion, the Wahhabi doctrines were strictly guided by the Qoran and the traditions of the Prophet, and Muslim theologians could find little fault with them. But in the practical application of their principles, the savagery of their massacres of other Muslims, their greed for loot and their iconoclastic destruction of tombs and holy places, caused them to be regarded with hatred and repulsion by other professors of the Islamic faith.*[16]Glubb's war with the Ikhwan of the Nejed lasted a decade. And as he wrote of its end, "The fanatical Ikhwan movement has vanished, though the people of Nejed are still Wahhabis."[17]What was true in 1930 is true today.

Saudi Arabia's Current Wahhabism

Where Matthew Gray and other analysts go wrong is in believing that because Saudi Arabia as a "rentier" state is the only reason it does not offer "…concessions to society such as a democratic bargain or a development strategy" to its people. The real reason is because Islamic ideol-

---

14 Id.

15 Id. at 110.

16 Glubb, "War in the Desert," Hodder and Stoughton (1960), p.47.

17 Id. at 344.

ogy—more specifically Wahhabist ideology—establishes a very different "social contract" than that envisioned by Jean Jacques Rousseau in 1762.

In his essay on the social contract, Rousseau wrote that its object was, "'To find a form of association which may defend and protect with the whole force of the community the person and property of every associate, and by means of which each, coalescing with all, may nevertheless obey only himself, and remain as free as before.' Such is the fundamental problem of which the social contract furnishes the solution."[18] At the risk of oversimplifying Rousseau, the social contract is meant to preserve individual freedom to the greatest degree that doesn't interfere with the ability of the state to protect its citizens. Rousseau's formulation is minimalist: the individual surrenders the least amount of personal freedom to make a form of government possible.

The Wahhabist social contract is the antithesis of Rousseau's formulation.

A contemporary of Rousseau, Muhamad ibn Abdul Wahhab, (1703?–1792) created a Sunni Muslim sect that is, as the Congressional Research Service labeled it, "puritanical."[19] Strictly applied in Saudi Arabia, the Wahhabist ideology seeks to purify Islam of any innovations, practices or beliefs that aren't contained in the Seventh Century teachings of Mohammed and his companions.[20] In 1963, King Faisal gave Wahhabi religious leaders control over the Saudi education system.[21] This may have done more to institutionalize Wahhabi ideology than any other act of his reign.

Saudi Arabia has no constitution. In 1992, the monarchy promulgated the nation's "Basic Law" which sets out its terms of rule.[22]

Islam—especially as it is believed by Wahhabis—is not only a religion but also an ideology. And nowhere is this as clear as in the Saudi Basic Law. This law is nothing more or less than Saudi Arabia's implementation of fundamentalist, intolerant, puritanical Wahhabism.

---

[18] http://chnm.gmu.edu/revolution/d/275/

[19] CRS, "The Islamic Traditions of Wahhabism and Salafiya," Report 21695, January 2008.

[20] Id.

[21] Gold, "Hatred's Kingdom," (Regnery 2003), p.77.

[22] http://www.saudiembassy.net/about/country-information/laws/The_Basic_Law_Of_Governance.aspx

Article 1 of the Basic Law states, "The Kingdom of Saudi Arabia is a sovereign Arab Islamic State. Its religion is Islam. Its constitution is Almighty God's Book, The Holy Qur'an, and the Sunna (Traditions) of the Prophet (PBUH). Arabic is the language of the Kingdom. The City of Riyadh is the capital."[23]There are no freedoms of speech, religion, the press, assembly, to keep and bear arms or any of the other rights Americans enjoy. In their place, Islam and Sharia law are substituted.

Citizens are required to pledge allegiance to the king (Article 6) and, Article 7 states, "Government in the Kingdom of Saudi Arabia derives its authority from the Book of God and the Sunna of the Prophet (PBUH), which are the ultimate sources of reference for this Law and the other laws of the State."

This is the central ideological connection between religion and government. Ideology, after all, is an integrated set of beliefs upon which a system of government is intended to be based. The puritanical Wahhabi sect is thus institutionalized as Saudi Arabia's government. The nation's economy, its culture and its social contract are molded into conformity with Wahhabi beliefs.

Thus, dissent is prohibited in the Basic Law (Article 12), the State is compelled to propagate Islam (Article 23), and the media are specifically restrained so that they are prohibited from promoting disorder or division affecting the state or its "public relations." (Article 39). It is as if the characters from the television show "Mad Men" held constitutional office and there were legal penalties for questioning their ad campaigns.

Saudi Arabia's Wahhabi fundamentalism has created a society that is both wealthy beyond imagination and entirely dismissive of the humanity of other races, nationalities and religions. This is evidenced in its treatment of such people who fall under its control. As the CIA World Factbook summarizes their condition:

Saudi Arabia is a destination country for men and women subjected to forced labor and, to a lesser extent, forced prostitution; men and women from Bangladesh, India, Sri Lanka, Nepal, Pakistan, the Philippines, Indonesia, Sudan, Ethiopia, Kenya, and many other countries voluntarily travel to Saudi Arabia as domestic

---

[23] Id.

servants or other low-skilled laborers, but some subsequently face conditions indicative of involuntary servitude (many are forced to work months or years beyond their contract term because employers withhold passports and required exit visas); women, primarily from Asian and African countries, are believed to be forced into prostitution in Saudi Arabia; others were reportedly kidnapped and forced into prostitution after running away from abusive employers; Yemeni, Nigerian, Pakistani, Afghan, Chadian, and Sudanese children were subjected to forced labor as beggars and street vendors in Saudi Arabia, facilitated by criminal gangs.[24]The most salient fact these people have in common is that they are not Wahhabi Muslims. (They are also not Westerners or East Asians whose governments are capable of protecting them.) In effect, they become slaves for however long they may remain in Saudi Arabia.

Saudi Funding of Terrorism: Protection Money and Spreading Wahabbism

The principle competence of the Saudi government is spending money. How it does so—and wishes to do in places within its borders but outside its control—says a great deal about the survival instincts of its ruling elite.

Effective Saudi counterintelligence is only one strategy the Saudi regime employs in defense against terrorism. Another is the evident attempt by the Saudis—including many members of the royal family—to pay "protection money" to terrorist groups in hope of buying immunity to attack. And in hope of spreading Wahhabism.

Under Article 23 of the Saudi Basic Law, the government is compelled to spread Wahhabist Islam. One of the ways it does so is sponsoring terrorism. Another is to spread Wahhabist ideology by sponsoring schools—Wahhabist madrassas—around the world from the United States to Pakistan.

In a June 2013 report, the European Parliament issued the results of its study of Saudi Arabian sponsorship of terrorism around the world.[25]

---

24   CIA World Factbook, supra.

25   "The Involvement of Salafism/Wahhabism in the Support and Supply of Arms to Rebel Groups Around the World," Directorate-General for External Policies, (https://docs.

The EU Parliament chose to study four regions of the world: South and Southeast Asia (Afghanistan, Pakistan, Indonesia and the Philippines), Syria, North Africa and the Sahel.

In South and Southeast Asia, the report labels Saudi Arabia as a major source of funding for terrorist and rebel organizations since the 1970s. In Afghanistan, the report says, the Saudis' proxy war undertaken in response to the Soviet invasion was, "…an occasion to affirm Wahhabism as the 'true belief' in sharp contrast to the atheism promoted by 'infidel' communists and the 'deviating' Islam followed by Sufis and Shiites."[26]In Pakistan, the report states, Saudi Arabia operated madrassas—religious schools—to recruit jihadis to fight the Soviets. They were highly successful: among the people who studied at their madrassas were Mullah Omar, founder of the Taliban and Jallaludin Haqqani, founder of the terrorist Haqqani network.[27] The Taliban and the Haqqani network continue to be the main opposition forces to both the Karzai government in Afghanistan and the Pakistani government.

The Saudis established madrassas for the Deobandi and Wahhabist ideologies in many villages around Pakistan, recruiting young men and children who were sent to the Pakistani "Federally-administered tribal areas" for further training and to fight.[28]In Indonesia, the EU report links Saudi funding of Islamic "charities" to funding al-Qaida.

The problem of Saudi funding of terrorism is one of the most widely-known and least discussed in American politics. In fact, the U.S. government goes to great lengths to prevent it being discussed such as classifying any official communication that contains the facts that are widely known.

In a 30 December 2009 secret cable to all embassies, divulged by Wikileaks, the U.S. State Department wrote:

"(S/NF) While the Kingdom of Saudi Arabia (KSA) takes seriously the threat of terrorism within Saudi Arabia, it has been an ongoing

---

google.com/viewer?a=v&pid=sites&srcid=ZGVmYXVsdGRvbWFpbnxoYWlkZXJub3Rlc3 xneDo3NDE0wMDI3NjViZTNjODZm)

[26] Id.

[27] Id.

[28] In a meeting in September 2008, a senior Bush Administration national security official told me that there were over half a million jihadi fighters in the FATA region.

challenge to persuade Saudi officials to treat terrorist financing emanating from Saudi Arabia as a strategic priority. Due in part to intense focus by the USG over the last several years, Saudi Arabia has begun to make important progress on this front and has responded to terrorist financing concerns raised by the United States through proactively investigating and detaining financial facilitators of concern. Still, donors in Saudi Arabia constitute the most significant source of funding to Sunni terrorist groups worldwide…

"(S/NF) The USG engages regularly with the Saudi Government on terrorist financing. The establishment in 2008 of a Treasury attaché office presence in Riyadh contributes to robust interaction and information sharing on the issue. *Despite this presence, however, more needs to be done since Saudi Arabia remains a critical financial support base for al-Qa'ida, the Taliban, LeT, and other terrorist groups, including Hamas, which probably raise millions of dollars annually from Saudi sources, often during Hajj and Ramadan. In contrast to its increasingly aggressive efforts to disrupt al-Qa'ida's access to funding from Saudi sources, Riyadh has taken only limited action to disrupt fundraising for the UN 1267-listed Taliban and LeT-groups that are also aligned with al-Qa'ida and focused on undermining stability in Afghanistan and Pakistan.*[29] So far, there is no independent proof that sponsorship of terrorism is or is not a policy of the Saudi government. It may well be that the government merely tolerates private financing of terror, or it could just as easily be that the government regards the private funding of terror with approval and as a convenient substitute for affirmative, traceable government action.

But, at least so far, the strategy of paying "protection money" to terrorist groups appears to be working. Though many Sunni–Salafist groups such as al-Qaida proclaim the Saudi royal family to be their mortal enemies, the attacks on Saudi targets have not been as large or successful as

---

[29] http://www.theguardian.com/world/us-embassy-cables-documents/242073. "S/NF" means "Secret/No Dissemination to Foreign Governments."

attacks on American and other Western targets. Insofar as those groups are concerned, they are unlikely to be creating crises in Saudi Arabia within the next three to five years.

The same cannot be said for other terrorist groups which are more clearly dependent on the sponsorship of nations, and those who may be turned to terrorism and revolt by their Shiite co-religionists in Iran.

Threats to Saudi Stability

Short term threats to Saudi stability are primarily economic and societal. They range from a sudden diminution of or disruption to the oil market to threats to the regime coming from the populace. And there are other threats, far more serious, from neighboring nations.

Saudi Arabia and the other oil-rich Gulf States benefit from the largest transfer of wealth in the history of the world. If the price of oil remains, as it has for the past three years, at approximately $100/barrel, Saudi Arabia can count on payments of about $1.17 billion per day or $427.05 billion per year. (This is not a pure wealth transfer because the nations importing oil consume it, with varying levels of efficiency, to produce other kinds of wealth.)

The world's appetite for oil is undiminished. In fact, it is apparently growing due to the expansion of the Chinese economy. There is little likelihood that, in the three-to-five year period with which we are concerned, there will be any major market diminishment for Saudi oil.

But, as we shall see below, market disruption by nations other than Saudi Arabia is a significant possibility.

We should discount those "threats" which do not endanger the regime such as the Western media's preoccupation with women's rights issues including the right to drive. These are distractions which may be media obsessions from time to time, but they are not threats to the Saudi regime.

The three most important threats to the Saudi regime are: the eruption of riots and terrorism among the Shia minority; a possible upheaval during or soon after the advent of the next king; the threats from the Eastern Shia, and the threats emanating and Iran's ally, Syria and Iran itself.

An Unlikely Crisis of Succession

The age gap between the Saudi population and its royal rulers is enormous, perhaps the most pronounced in the world.

The age gap is significant, but the questions it creates are much more complicated than to ask whether the Saudi royal family is spending enough to buy the peace with the Wahhabi populace.

Born August 1, 1924, King Abdullah is nearing ninety years of age. Reports of his ill-health vary wildly.[30] He has already outlived two chosen successors, Princes Nayef and Sultan.

What happens after Abdullah dies or retires will determine whether and how the Saudi gerontocracy remains in power. The policies pursued by the next generation of Saudi leaders will almost certainly determine whether a crisis results from the succession.

Abdullah has undertaken some reforms aimed at ameliorating any restiveness in the younger population. Saudi television, like the Saudi press, is still government controlled. But since about 2010, according to a businessman who frequently travels to Saudi Arabia, it's now a commonplace to see scantily-clad women on television. That would have been unimaginable only a few years ago. Similarly, only two or three years ago, Saudi security forces or police were visible on almost every street corner. Now, they are far less visible.

Social unrest among Saudi Arabia's Wahhabi majority appears to be minimal and the royal family is spending a great deal of money to keep it so. Saudi Arabia's government revenues are about $326.5 billion a year and its expenditures are estimated (for 2012) at $234.8 billion. Since the eruption of the so-called "Arab Spring" in 2011, King Abdullah committed to spend about $130 billion on public benefits including education benefits, unemployment allowances, higher wages and low-income housing.[31]But the news isn't all good. The Saudis apparently want to be self-sufficient in less than twenty years. To do that, they will have to do a lot more to educate their people. One

---

[30] On report in October 2013 claimed the king was clinically dead. http://www.presstv.com/detail/2013/05/26/305584/saudi-arabias-king-clinically-dead/

[31] F. Gregory Gause, "Is Saudi Arabia Stable?", Cairo Review of Global Affairs, 10 September 2013, (http://www.aucegypt.edu/gapp/cairoreview/pages/articleDetails.aspx?aid=424)

Ages of leaders and led

Years

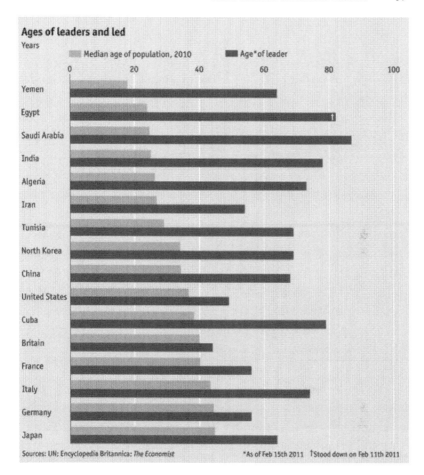

■ Median age of population, 2010   ■ Age* of leader

0   20   40   60   80   100

Yemen
Egypt
Saudi Arabia
India
Algeria
Iran
Tunisia
North Korea
China
United States
Cuba
Britain
France
Italy
Germany
Japan

Sources: UN; Encyclopedia Britannica; *The Economist*   *As of Feb 15th 2011 †Stood down on Feb 11th 2011

expert described the Saudis' demographic problems vividly: they have raised an unproductive generation that is too used to relying on the state for support. The Saudis' dream of self-sufficiency is currently thwarted by an inability to provide themselves with health care, technology and engineering expertise. There is no cultural outflow of either literature or music.

And there is an "urbanization" problem. While the urban population is too unproductive, the rural population is too divorced from the Saudi mainstream. With respect to the Shiites in the Eastern area, that lack of a connection contains a considerable threat.

The "next" generation of Saudi leaders is really a continuation of the one that rules the nation now. It is still far older than the average Saudi. Crown Prince Salman (who also serves as minister of defense) is about 78, Prince Muqrin—third in line to the throne—is 68. Muqrin is a long-time favorite of Abdullah and often accompanies him on trips.[32] It is highly unlikely that either Salman or Muqrin would deviate significantly from Abdullah's social policies, so dissatisfaction with either is not at all likely to stir up enough domestic unrest as to threaten the regime.

When Salman and Muqrin's sub-generation passes, Saudi succession will become problematic. Though it is beyond the scope of this study, the possibility of regime change looms large beyond the five-year outlook. Not only will the Saudis themselves make it so, but there will be many other nations—from Iran to China and more—that will employ diplomatic and perhaps military power to influence or control the succession.

The Eastern Shia Minority

The primary domestic threat to the Saudi regime isn't from young Wahhabis: it is from an increasingly restive and potentially violent Shia minority, primarily in Saudi Arabia's eastern province.

This is the source of the Saudi regime's greatest fear. And with good reason.

Since the March 2011 "day of rage," in which government opponents planned but did not succeed in turning out massive demonstrations, sporadic but persistent demonstrations have occurred in Saudi Arabia, some violent. After July 2012, when Saudi forces shot and then imprisoned Shia cleric Sheikh Nimr al-Nimr, the Shia of Eastern Saudi Arabia have become more and more volatile. In demonstrations against his arrest, three died.[33] According to one report, the Saudi regime holds about 30,000 political prisoners, including an unknown number of Shia.[34] The common wisdom among most westerners is that most Saudi Shia apparently remains loyal to the Saudi regime. If that is true at all, that loyalty

---

32 http://www.thedailybeast.com/articles/2013/02/03/with-prince-muqrin-s-appointment-saudi-succession-crisis-looms.html

33 http://www.presstv.com/detail/2013/03/26/295276/saudi-cleric-charged-with-inciting-unrest/

34 Id.

is very shallow. And it is subject to a great shift which may happen in the next three to five years.

In the southeastern area of Saudi Arabia, where these people live near the border with Yemen, is an area already beset by a proxy war the Saudis are fighting with Iran. Allied with the Saudis are the UAE and Qatar. But Iran is intervening in Saudi Arabia to reach its Shiite co-religionists. And it is succeeding.

The area bordering Yemen is primarily tribal, without a functioning arm of the Saudi government. What the Saudis fear is precisely what is happening today: the Iranians are spreading their influence through the region by allying with some of the tribes and pouring resources—money, arms and probably troops of the Iranian Revolutionary Guard Corps— into the area. The only restraint the Iranians suffer is the level of resources their economy can provide.

The Saudis would like to inject their own government there, to provide schools, hospitals and other resources people would expect a government to provide. That they haven't been able to do so—and there is no evidence even of an effective plan to do so—reflects very badly on the Saudi government. If its principle competence is spending money, and it cannot spend effectively to create a more beneficial government presence in the troubled area, that is a condition that could propel an insurgency against the Saudi government.[35]

The Saudi Shiites are an ignition point. If the Iranians can pour enough fuel on their fire, the entire nation could see an upsurge in terrorist violence that not even the otherwise capable Saudi intelligence and counterterrorism forces would be able to control. Were enough radical Shia clerics to be present to inflame the local tribes, and if the IRGC were to gain a better foothold, the Saudi regime could suffer a fatal crisis.

As shown below, Saudi Arabia's interventions, not only in the Syrian civil war but also against Bahraini Shiites in 2011, are certain to lead to Iranian support for Saudi Shia protests and riots. (It is a mistake to assume that the Saudi intervention in Syria, discussed below, would be the only cause of the Iranian intervention among the Saudi Shiites. The

[35] *See, e.g.,* Galula, "Counterinsurgency Warfare: Theory and Practice," (1960) (reprinted by PSI Classics)

two nations have been enemies since Saudi Arabia was founded. Saudi intervention on the side of Iraq in the 1980–1988 Iran–Iraq war is still a fresh memory in Iran. The Saudi intervention in Syria is only the most recent reopening of the old wound.)

This is the most likely threat to the Saudi regime in the next three to five years. Though other threats may seem to loom larger, this is the one that the Saudis fear most. And the one that is least likely to be lessened or eliminated by anyone outside of Saudi Arabia.

It is not so long ago—in 1975—that King Faisal was assassinated by a member of the royal family. Given Iran's ability to finance and support logistically terrorist acts in Saudi Arabia, such acts are quite likely within the next three to five years. They have the potential to destabilize not only Saudi Arabia's royal family but oil production as well.

Other Threats

Iran—and its proxy war in Syria that the Saudis oppose—give rise the two existential threats the Saudis face in the next three to five years.

Iran's development of nuclear weapons is the biggest threat the Saudis face. So far, they have chosen to oppose Iran by intervening—as they did in Bahrain—on the side of Sunni Muslims against Shia. And they have chosen to fight proxy wars against Iran as in Syria for example.

Syria is the most important conflict the Saudis have engaged in openly since America led the coalition to throw Saddam Hussein's forces out of Kuwait in 1990. The Saudis prefer—at least so far—to fight Iran in Syria using proxy forces.

The Saudis are committed to toppling Syria's Assad regime. In what he believed at the time was a key to the Saudi strategy, King Abdullah appointed Prince Bandar—former ambassador to Washington—to lead the effort to overthrow Bashar Assad's regime, and turned Adel al-Jubeir—the current ambassador to the US—loose to lobby congress for American intervention.[36]

Saudi funding and arms shipments, added to those of other Arab states—notably Qatar—have been flowing to the Syrian rebels since at

---

[36] *Wall Street Journal*, August 25, 2013.

least February 2013. This Arab investment in Syria's civil war makes Saudi Arabia a principal opponent to Iran in that war.

Iran has not only sent arms and funding to Assad, it has also sent Iranian Revolutionary Guard troops to fight alongside the Assad regime's forces. Additionally, Iran has trained thousands of Shiite fighters from Iraq and other nations to fight for Assad.[37] Russia has sent Assad arms and funding as well.

Saudi Arabia regards the Assad regime as a destabilizing Iranian proxy on its border, a correct perception. Events in September and October 2013 have substantially weakened Saudi Arabia's position in Syria. President Obama's acceptance of the deal offered by Russian President Putin, mooting the threat of American military intervention in Syria, was disastrous for the Saudis. They believe they are being surrounded by Iranian allies—Shiites loyal to Iran—in Lebanon (the very large Hizballah terrorist group), Yemen, Bahrain and Iraq.[38]

So seriously do the Saudis regard the threat emanating from the Syrian civil war that they rejected a seat on the UN Security Council on 18 October 2013. The principal reason given for the rejection was the Security Council's failure to bring the Syrian civil war to an end. It would have been the first time the Saudis held a Security Council seat.[39] The Saudis' rejection of the Security Council seat was unprecedented in UN history and especially surprising since the Saudis had campaigned for the seat up until the time it was chosen.[40] That they did so indicates that they were planning to reject the seat for some time before the election.

President Obama has placed the UN Security Council squarely in charge of the question of how, if at all, the non-Arab states (except for Israel) will deal with Iran's nuclear weapons program. The Saudi rejection of the Security Council seat amounts to a diplomatic proclamation of their contempt for the UN's and America's powerlessness in the

---

[37] *Wall Street Journal*, Sept. 16, 2013, (http://online.wsj.com/article/SB100014241278 873238646045790067382861808984.html)

[38] *Financial Times*, October 6, 2013, http://www.ft.com/intl/cms/s/0/e4cc1f30-2b4e-11e3-a1b7-00144feab7de.html#axzz2hWJgCdpx

[39] *Washington Post*, October 19, 2013, (http://www.washingtonpost.com/world/saudi-arabia-rejects-seat-on-un-security-council/2013/10/18/9d9ae476-3813-11e3-ae46-e4248e75c8ea_story.html)

[40] Id.

Middle East. Add to that the fact that if Saudi Arabia took the Security Council seat, it would have had to vote on the questions of Iran's nuclear program and the continuation or relaxation of sanctions on Iran.[41] The fact that Saudi Arabia wanted to escape that responsibility is another indication of Saudi Arabia's evident view of the failure of American diplomacy.

The Saudis' rejection of the UN Security Council seat was a major signal of their frustration with President Obama's diplomatic efforts not only against Assad, but also his futile efforts in the Israeli–Palestinian conflict and in dealing with the Iran nuclear weapons program. Particularly objectionable to them was Obama's willingness to follow Putin's plan that ensures Assad will remain in power for the foreseeable future and will not deprive him of his chemical weapons.

The weekend after the U.N. rejection, Prince Bandar—the leader of the Saudi effort to topple Assad—reportedly called diplomats to Jeddah to express the Saudis displeasure with the Obama administration. Bandar was quoted as telling the diplomats, "This was a message for the U.S., not the U.N."[42]

And only days later, the American-Saudi gap grew wider. The Saudis, not satisfied with the results of their rejection of the UN Security Council, began to hint at economic consequences for the U.S. Though Secretary of State John Kerry assured the Saudis that he believed no deal with Iran was better than a bad deal, Prince Bandar told diplomats that he planned to reduce diplomatic interaction with the U.S.[43]

The evident power vacuum in the Middle East caused by Obama's default to Putin and no-conditions diplomatic engagement with Iran will not remain empty for long. Iran is undoubtedly performing a real-time analysis and reconnaissance of Saudi Arabia, aiming to respond to the Saudi war-by-proxy against Bashar Assad. Iran's Shiite kakistocracy is

---

[41] This was alluded to in an article in the government-controlled *Arab News* that appeared two days after the rejection. (http://www.arabnews.com/news/468253)

[42] *Wall Street Journal*, October 22, 2013, (http://online.wsj.com/news/articles/SB10001 424052702303902404579150011732240016?mod=WSJ_hps_LEFTTopStories)

[43] http://www.dailymail.co.uk/news/article-2472680/Saudi-Arabia-severs-diplomatic-ties-US-response-conflict-Syria.html

certain to respond to Saudi Arabia's intervention in Syria. Given the two nations' lasting enmity, the questions are how and when, not if.

Iran has been highly successful in stirring up Iraq's Shiite population to fight against Americans while they were in Iraq and now for Assad in Syria. Though the Saudi Shia population is reportedly still loyal to the Saudi regime, that could change rapidly as a result of Iranian intervention. Any surge of terrorist violence from Saudi Arabia's Shiite minority would be put down ruthlessly by Saudi forces.

That ruthlessness—as the Soviet invasion of Afghanistan proved—would enable Iran to further inflame the Saudi Shiites and, over time, could turn eastern Saudi Arabia into an area resembling the deadly "Sunni Triangle" in Iraq which was a hotbed of jihadist terrorism.

Iran will see, and likely act upon, the opportunity that the Saudi succession gives it to manufacture a crisis in Saudi Arabia to take revenge for the intervention in Syria. Timing its response, quite possibly combining terrorist attacks with cyber attacks, must be expected and planned for.

When Would Iran Act, and How?

Iran's seeming preoccupation with relief from UN sanctions and the possibility of a deal with America regarding its nuclear weapons program will not preclude more aggressive Iranian action when King Abdullah dies or if it becomes clear that Assad were in imminent danger of losing and being removed from power in the Syrian civil war.

If there is proximity in time between the two events the Iranians could act to combine them for political and historical purposes.

The reason that the nuclear negotiations may provide no respite for the Saudis is that the West's negotiating team—the UN's so-called "Perm Five + 1", the five permanent members of the UN Security Council plus Germany—have made a fundamental misjudgment of what is at stake in the negotiations.

The Perm 5 + 1 mistakenly believe that peace—at least nuclear disarmament of Iran—can be gained in those negotiations. Iran has made it clear that it will not give up its nuclear ambitions and will not even concede any limitation of its "right" to enrich uranium. There is no evidence that Iran has the same beliefs as do its interlocutors. In fact, it certainly believes that the negotiations are a means to other ends.

Iran has used previous rounds of negotiations with Western powers simply to give it more time to continue its development of nuclear weapons. There is no reason to believe that this is not Iran's intent in this round of talks.

Iran's low regard for the negotiations is matched by America's too-high expectations. After the first day of meetings the Iranian negotiator said the Western powers were more eager for an agreement than he was.[44] In that context, Iran must believe that it can take risks in Saudi Arabia regardless of the nuclear talks.

Iran is proving itself a quick study. When President Obama's threat of military action in Syria was easily suborned by Russian President Putin's "plan" for disarming Syria's chemical weapons capabilities, Iran was quick to follow along, adapting Putin's model to its own purposes.

Iran has not, for one moment, slowed or stopped its development of nuclear weapons since about 1981.

In fact, when Iranian President Rouhani embraced the new negotiations in his speech at the UN, he swore that Iran has never chosen "deceit and secrecy" when in fact deceit and secrecy have been the norm. In a speech that followed Rouhani's by several days, Israeli Prime Minister Netanyahu pointed out that Iran was caught in 2002 and 2009 secretly building uranium enrichment facilities in Natanz and Qom.[45]

In 2003, Iran told the UN's "nuclear watchdog"—the International Atomic Energy Agency—that it intended to build a heavy water reactor in Arak. Operation of the Arak reactor may begin as early as 2014. The reactor can be used to produce weapons-grade plutonium.[46] In 2009, the *Times of London* reported that Iran was developing trigger-

---

[44] http://www.nydailynews.com/news/politics/kerry-constructive-meeting-iran-article-1.1469024

[45] http://www.timesofisrael.com/full-text-netanyahus-2013-speech-to-the-un-general-assembly/

[46] http://carnegieeurope.eu/2013/09/12/in-heavy-water-iran-s-potential-plutonium-production/gnf3

ing devices for nuclear weapons.[47] Further reporting revealed that this effort dated back to at least 2005.[48] Then, as now, Iran denied it was developing nuclear weapons.

With that track record, it is impossible to credit Iran's claimed desire to compromise its nuclear ambitions. Again, the West has mistaken its intent. Which, in Saudi terms, leaves Iran undeterred from retaliating for the Saudi interference in Syria.

It is unlikely that Iran will act openly against Saudi Arabia until they obtain deployable (i.e., deliverable by missile) nuclear weapons. However, if the Syrian civil war's end is suddenly in sight, and the likely outcome a toppling of the Assad regime, Iran's stake in that conflict might compel it to act covertly.

Both the public advent of a nuclear-armed Iran and a decisive moment in the Syrian civil war are very likely to occur within the next three to five years.

The Iranians are not likely to use nuclear weapons against Saudi Arabia. They want to control Saudi, its wealth and oil exports, not destroy them. Further, the Saudi cities of Mecca and Medina are holy to all Muslims, so the Iranians—even if they decided to bomb Riyadh—would almost certainly refrain from mounting a nuclear attack on Saudi Arabia.

The counterpart of this is the possibility that the Saudis could obtain their own nuclear weapons as some sort of deterrent against Iran. There are reports that the Saudis have already requested that Pakistan make several nuclear weapons for the Saudis, but while possible that is a bit far-fetched. First, the possibility of deterring Iran is not great (given its Shiite ideology) and second, a nuclear-armed Saudi Arabia could provoke the Iranians to an attack they might otherwise not contemplate. Third, the Saudi air force—at this point—lacks the missiles and long-range nuclear-capable aircraft to deliver such weapons. Should they buy such weapons (and their recent purchase of new F-15s from the United

---

[47] http://www.thetimes.co.uk/tto/news/world/middleeast/article2605586.ece

[48] http://www.telegraph.co.uk/news/worldnews/middleeast/iran/6812089/Iran-accused-of-testing-nuclear-bomb-triggers.html

States could further that idea) the entire Middle East would plunge into a nuclear arms race.

There are several options that Iran can take to precipitate a crisis in Saudi succession ranging from the assassination of one or more likely successors to the king to large-scale terrorist attacks on the country's oil infrastructure to announcing completion of Iran's development of nuclear weapons.

These possible crises—which Iran can precipitate within the next three to five years—would be enough to affix the likelihood of a crisis that could result in the destabilization or even removal of the Saudi regime within the next three to five years were it not for the need to examine the other criteria established for this study. In those criteria are facts which may ameliorate or even prevent these crises which are discussed below. Other responses by Iran could be more immediately serious for the Saudi regime. Iran has often threatened to close the Straits of Hormuz, a move that would block Saudi oil shipments. Any effort to do so would be interdicted or remedied by the U.S. Fifth Fleet based in Bahrain, but the effort could succeed for some period of time.[49]

The threats of mobilizing Saudi Shias and closing the Straits are not to be taken lightly, but aren't—in our time frame—existential threats to the Saudi regime. There are two others. The first is Iran, the second may result from Saudi Arabia's informal policy of funding terrorism.

The latter is not sufficiently likely to be worthy of analysis here. Though terrorist groups of the Salafist-Sunni variety often proclaim the Saudi royal family as their enemy, their efforts against the Saudi royals have been neither significant nor frequent. From their record of actions, these terrorist groups appear to have chosen to make minor attacks against the Saudi royals sufficient only to maintaining the credibility of their threat, and not to truly pose an existential threat.

For the next three to five years, it is safe to project that as long as Saudi money continues to flow in an amount sufficient to maintain it as a pri-

---

49 See, e.g., *New York Times*, December 28, 2011. http://www.nytimes.com/2011/12/29/world/middleeast/noise-level-rises-over-iran-threat-to-close-strait-of-hormuz.html?_r=0

mary source of support for the groups, they will not pose a greater threat to Saudi stability than they do now.

2. Saudi Arabia's Alliances

In 1943, Franklin Roosevelt declared the defense of Saudi Arabia to be in America's national security interest. Since then, America has maintained a close alliance with the Saudi royal family and its military forces. Many if not all of the Saudi air force's pilots are American-trained. The Saudi military is mostly American-armed and trained.[50] The United States has used Saudi Arabia as a base for its forces several times, most notably in preparation for the 1991 Gulf War and again in preparation for the invasion of Iraq in 2003. In both cases, Saudi Arabia was not only the host to US forces, but an active military ally. Saudi air force aircraft flew attack missions against Iraqi forces from the first day of the 1991 Gulf War.

But there have been breaks in the relationship, most damaging being the OPEC oil boycott against the US after the 1973 Arab–Israeli war. The Saudis led the embargo and have alleged that the US threatened military action against them as a result.[51] The US has defended Israel from Arab aggression—with arms and aid verging on the use of military force— almost since Israel was founded. Nevertheless, the unwritten understanding based on Roosevelt's 1943 proclamation has been that the US would defend Saudi Arabia against all other enemies.

Other nations, including especially oil-dependent European nations, have aligned themselves with Saudi Arabia but none have as close military ties as does the United States.

Saudi Arabia's other alliances—the most significant of which are the Organization of Islamic Cooperation, the Organization of Petroleum Exporting Countries—are not military alliances. They are forums for economic cooperation and for the exercise of political influence globally.

---

[50] Metz, "Saudi Arabia: A country study," (1992) (http://countrystudies.us/saudi-arabia/59.htm)

[51] http://www.arabnews.com/node/311576

The Organization of Islamic Cooperation is a creature of the UN,[52] apparently aimed at presenting a moderate image of Islam to the world. Its charter is conspicuously absent from its website.

Typical of the OIC's activities is the resolution it sponsored and which was adopted by the General Assembly in November 2012.[53] The resolution proclaimed a consensus among the UN members to combat intolerance and discrimination based on religious belief. That resolution is consistent with earlier resolutions the OIC had offered which included the "defamation" of religions among the things it proclaimed against.[54] Those earlier versions had drawn opposition from Western states as an effort to make speech against Islam a crime. Saudi Arabia, as in other Islamic countries, has no freedom of speech and, in fact, prohibits it in its Basic Law.[55] In the case of the OIC, those least tolerant of other religions are persuading others to condemn intolerance. The OIC is, then, a propaganda arm of the Islamic states engaged in "disinformation" campaigns. "Disinformation" occurs when an original source of false information persuades others to re-publish the original falsehood.[56]

The Organization of Oil Exporting Countries—OPEC—is the most effective economic alliance the Saudis belong to, and by virtue of their oil production, the one they lead. It is perhaps the only one they will ever need. And perhaps not.

The Arab oil embargo, from October 1973 to March 1974, was meant to penalize the US for supporting Israel. It can be regarded as a failure because it did nothing to reduce that support. It did result in a spike in oil prices, but Americans were saving energy faster than OPEC nations could easily produce it.[57] Though America learned little from the OPEC embargo, the OPEC nations—especially Saudi Arabia— apparently learned a lot.

---

52 http://www.oicun.org/

53 http://www.oicun.org/9/20121211113814924.html

54 http://www.gatestoneinstitute.org/2767/islam-oic-thought-police

55 Note 22, above, in Articles 12, 23 and 39.

56 See "*Disinformation*," Pacepa and Rychlak, WND Books (2013).

57 Christian Science Monitor, October 17, 2013 (http://www.csmonitor.com/Environment/Energy-Voices/2013/1017/How-the-1973-oil-embargo-saved-energy)

As noted above, about fifty percent of Saudi oil went to the Far East in 2012.[58] And more will follow in the future.

In 2012, Saudi Aramco signed an agreement with the Chinese government-controlled company Sinotec to build a refinery in the town of Yanbu on the Red Sea. The refinery will have the capacity to process 400,000 barrels of oil a day, some or all of which will end up in China.[59]

The Chinese interest in Saudi Arabia may result in a quasi-economic-military alliance between the two nations. Chinese Premier Wen Jibao, visiting Saudi Arabia as his first stop in a 2012 tour of the Middle East, signed a series of agreements with Saudi Arabia described as *"An agreement between the two governments on the peaceful usage of nuclear energy."*

Wen also tried to persuade the Saudis to open their oil and gas industry to expanded Chinese investment[60] and, thus, to greater Chinese control. It is not clear that the Saudis have decided on China as their new protector/ally replacing the US, but it is clear they are shopping for one.

Saudi Arabia may be hedging its bets on Iran's nuclear weapons program. When Iran is believed to have obtained nuclear arms—and the means of delivering them—Saudi Arabia will have to choose between remaining under the protection of America's nuclear deterrent and having its own nuclear forces. That agreement with China may mean that nuclear cooperation is already underway aimed at arming Saudi Arabia with nuclear weapons.

Saudi Arabia's defense and stability is still in the United States' interest. It is also in China's best interest, and in the best interest of the other nations that rely on Saudi oil production to sustain their economies. That fact boils down to the military defense of Saudi Arabia from foreign aggression. But the fact that such aggression could be undertaken in many forms makes the question of when and how that defense would be implemented far from clear.

In the unlikely event that the aggression were open—for example, the Iranians trying to block the Straits of Hormuz—the solution would be

---

[58] Supra, note 5.

[59] http://www.dailyreckoning.com.au/how-the-energy-and-oil-alliance-between-china-and-saudi-is-growing/2012/01/16/

[60] http://www.reuters.com/article/2012/01/15/us-saudi-arabia-china-idUS-TRE80E00O20120115

quite clear, at least up to a point. The United States Navy would intervene and clear the Straits of Iranian forces.

And if the aggression were covert—for example, an Iranian-sponsored
terrorist campaign against the Saudi royals or Saudi oil facilities or both—
the US and China would probably be limited to sharing intelligence with
Saudi forces. Nevertheless, such attacks combined with sophisticated
cyberwar attacks (of which the Iranians are probably capable) could over-
whelm Saudi counterterrorist forces.[61]

Recent assassinations of Iranian nuclear scientists come at a time when
Iran is very close to producing nuclear weapons. The assassination of
the cyberwar chief may be an indication of the progress of Iran's cyberwar program. There is no motive to assassinate someone who is not
succeeding.

Iran, it must be remembered, was the target of one of the most
advanced cyberwar attacks yet revealed: the "Stuxnet" worm, originated
in the United States with Israeli assistance[62], caused Iranian uranium
enrichment centrifuges to run at excessive speed, causing major damage.

Since then, Iran has worked to develop its own cyberwar capabilities.
Judging from the assassination, this effort must be regarded as a significant threat by one or more governments. The Saudis—as well as Americans and Israelis—are logical targets for an Iranian cyber-attack.

But the US and Israel have been developing their cyberwar capabilities—defensive and offensive—for more than a decade. Whether the
Saudis are as advanced would determine whether Iran or some other
nation could significantly damage the Saudi defense or oil apparatuses
in the next few years.

A sufficient threat to the stability of Saudi Arabia's oil supply, and perhaps a sufficient threat to the royal family's reign, would almost certainly
cause an American military response. It is well within the realm of possibility that China would offer its forces in some support to defend the
oil and the regime.

---

61 The October 2013 assassination of Iran's cyberwar chief, Mojtada Ahmadi, (http://
www.telegraph.co.uk/news/worldnews/middleeast/iran/10350285/Iranian-cyber-warfare-
commander-shot-dead-in-suspected-assassination.html) may be an indirect indication of
how serious Iran's cyberwar effort is.

62 http://www.nytimes.com/2012/06/01/world/middleeast/obama-ordered-wave-of-
cyberattacks-against-iran.html

But how quickly a threat can be implemented—especially one that is partly or entirely covert in its implementation—will determine how well any American or Chinese response will fare. The quicker a threat can be turned into established fact, the lesser effect may be possible from any response.

Within the next three to five years, Iran—and its ally Syria—are the only nations which will have the motivation to attack or try to destabilize Saudi Arabia. The Saudis' allies, the US and China, are likely to engage in major efforts that would at least ameliorate, and possibly defeat, any Iranian overt or covert attack on Saudi Arabia in that period.

3. Saudi Arabia's Investment in National Security

Saudi Arabia's military spending, as a percentage of GDP, is the largest in the world.[63] The world's fourth-largest military budget—$52.9 billion in 2013—[64] has produced a Saudi military of considerable strength. For example, the Saudi Air Force has over 300 combat aircraft including relatively 129 recent F-15s as well as tanker and special mission aircraft.[65] Its personnel strength is probably over 25,000 and it operates combat aircraft from at least four airfields.[66] The Saudi military numbers over 200,000 active duty personnel and its army is partially supported by domestic manufacture of armored vehicles.[67] The Saudi military benefits from American military training, weapon system sales and much more. The US has limited sales of missiles to Saudi Arabia to short-range non-ballistic missiles because they could be used against Israel. The Saudis have not made much progress, in recent years, in missile development. Its only ballistic missile is the 1980s-vintage Chinese Dong Feng-3 intermediate-range ballistic missile. *IHS Jane's 360* reports that the Saudis have recently improved some of their launch sites for its old—and, frankly, obsolescent—DF-3 nuclear-capable missiles.[68]

---

[63] http://www.economist.com/blogs/dailychart/2011/03/defence_budgets

[64] http://uk.finance.yahoo.com/news/saudi-arabian-defence-industry-placed-000000421.html

[65] www.flightglobal.com, "World Air Forces 2013."

[66] http://www.globalsecurity.org/military/world/gulf/rsaf.htm

[67] http://uk.finance.yahoo.com/news/saudi-arabian-defence-industry-placed-000000421.html

[68] http://www.janes.com/article/24321/saudi-ballistic-missile-site-revealed

Since the 1979 seizure Mecca's Grand Mosque, the Saudis have developed highly skilled counterterrorism capabilities. Concomitantly, the Saudi intelligence community—especially its General Security Service, its principal Intelligence service—is highly capable.

The Saudis have great confidence in their "elint"—NSA-like electronic intelligence—and "humint"—i.e., spy—capabilities.

That confidence, for now, appears well-justified. Their growth in capabilities is, as several sources report, part of their reaction to American policy in Iraq which Saudis believe could not be worse. The Saudis believe that their capabilities need to grow in direct proportion to their diminishing reliance on America's. Saudis, with good reason, see America as the reason Iraq is now ruled by its Shiite minority in close alliance with Iran.

Saudi Arabia certainly cannot be classified, unlike most of the NATO nations, as an ally that refuses to invest in its own defense. Saudi Arabia, however, is caught in its own policy dilemma. The more it is seen as siding with the United States—when the US is growing weaker in its ability to influence Saudi Arabia's neighboring states—the less Saudi Arabia will can assert itself as America's ally, particularly in respect to other Sunni Muslim states. At the same time, the Saudis will have to find other customers for their oil as America grows in its ability to produce oil and gas.

In short, what this means is that while the Saudis' ability to defend themselves is sustainable, its alliance with the United States may not be. China's influence with the Saudis will increase as does their economy's ability to purchase Saudi oil.

4. Saudi Arabia's Ability to Project Power

The US Navy is rightly proud to call each of its Nimitz-class aircraft carriers "98,000 tons of diplomacy." When the term "power projection" is used, that is its normal meaning. When a carrier battle group—which may consist of a dozen ships and submarines—is dispatched to a trouble spot, an American military presence is quickly felt.

For Saudi Arabia, power projection comes in two very different categories.

The first is the formal projection of military forces beyond the country's borders. The second is the constant effort in accordance with Saudi Arabia's basic law to spread the Wahhabist brand of Islam to every country.

In March 2011, about 1200 Saudi troops and another 800 from the United Arab Emirates entered Bahrain to help the government put down riots among its Shiite minority.[69] Iran reacted immediately, calling the troop movement an invasion and Bahraini Shiites called it an occupation.[70]

For the Saudis, this was not entirely an unusual action. Saudi Arabia has stationed troops in nearby countries and participated in the Arab-Israeli wars in 1967 and 1973. About 200,000 Saudi troops were stationed in Jordan in 1967 and about 3,000 fought the Israelis on the Syrian border in 1973.[71] Saudi air and ground forces fought as part of the US coalition in the 1991 Gulf War.

The Bahrain deployment was unusual, however, because it was accomplished for the specific purpose of opposing Shiites supported by Iran. It marked a new-found audacity in Saudi Arabia's use of military power.

In short, the Saudis have the ability to perform some power projection. Their air forces, supported by a few tanker aircraft, have a long range (non-nuclear) strike capability. Their ground forces, equipped with good vehicles and small arms are also relatively capable. Their shortfall is in staying power. It is very unlikely that the Saudi forces could accomplish a classic US-like projection of power for more than a few weeks without outside help.

The other form of power projection is the Saudis' relentless efforts to spread Wahhabism by sponsoring mosques and religious schools—madrassas—in other nations.

Charitable giving—known in Islam as "zakat"—is used by the Saudis to spread Wahhabism around the world. As the 9-11 Commission's report said:

---

[69] http://www.nytimes.com/2011/03/15/world/middleeast/15bahrain.html?pagewanted=all

[70] Id.

[71] http://www.saudidefence.com/saudi-arabian-army/

While Saudi charities are regulated by the Ministry of Labor and Social Welfare, charities and international relief agencies such as the World Assembly of Muslim Youth (WAMY) are currently regulated by the Ministry of Islamic Affairs. The ministry uses zakat and government funds to spread Wahhabi beliefs throughout the world, including in mosques and schools. Often these schools provide the only education available; even in affluent countries Saudi-funded Wahhabi schools are often the only Islamic schools. Some Wahhabi-funded organizations have been exploited by extremists to further their goal of violent jihad against non-Muslims.[72] Many of the mosques in the United States are funded by Saudi Arabia and must be presumed to be a part of the Saudis' effort to spread Wahhabism. And such mosques are a commonplace in the world. From Britain to Pakistan, Saudi Wahhabist mosques have proliferated under the Saudis' financial umbrella.[73] And in the United States, Saudi-Wahhabi mosques and schools are becoming common as well. The mosque attended by the Tsarnaev brothers—the Boston Marathon bombers—was half-funded by the Saudis.[74] The Saudis ability to project power, then, has to be measured not only by their ability to send military forces abroad but also by their long-term ambitions to spread their ideology-cum-religion around the world. If their Basic Law is to be taken at face value—that the State is obligated to propagate Islam[75]—that is a duty to project the ideology, and thus the power, of the Wahhabi sect to every corner of the world.

5. Strategic/Economic Security Assessment

Saudi Arabia occupies two pinnacles of power: first, as the nation that holds Mecca and Medina, it occupies a special place in Islam. No other

---

72 9-11 Commission Report, National Commission on Terrorist Attacks, (Norton 2011), p. 372

73 In June 2013, Saudi Arabia's deputy ambassador to Pakistan announced the funding of 100 more mosques in Pakistan. (http://www.pakistantoday.com.pk/2013/06/08/city/islamabad/saudi-arabias-gift-to-pakistan-100-mosques-100-wells-2000-eye-surgeries/)

74 http://www.usatoday.com/story/news/nation/2013/04/23/boston-mosque-radicals/2101411/

75 See Basic Law, Article 23

nation benefits from the religious imperative of the pilgrimage to Mecca; second, it sits atop a huge reserve of oil that seemingly ensures its prosperity for an indefinite time.

But there are influences, positive and negative, that will affect Saudi stability in the next three to five years. This study has reviewed the principal threats from the outflow of the Syrian civil war and from Iran both directly and indirectly. Those threats are sufficient to destabilize Saudi Arabia if one or both—in conjunction with other threats we have also named—are brought to bear singly or in combination.

One we have not yet considered is the effect of Saudi Arabia's growing disaffection with the United States.

There may come a time at which the Saudis are so fractured from the U.S. that they would divert the sale of their oil to other customers, effectively re-establishing the 1973–1974 oil embargo. But that is unlikely in the extreme, especially in the next three to five years.

What is far more likely, given the Saudis' economic interest, is that they will help the Chinese in their effort to weaken the dollar by accepting the renminbi as a "reserve currency." (A reserve currency is supposedly the safest from deflation or default, resulting in nations holding their foreign trade assets and accounts in that currency. The dollar has been a reserve currency for most of the world since World War II.)

On October 17, 2013 the Chinese credit agency Dagong downgraded the US's credit rating to A− and maintained its negative outlook for the dollar.[76] The stated reasons were the continuing risk of default by the US on its debt, and included a call for the world to consider building a de-Americanized world.[77] China's maneuver is clearly not altruistic, and has at its base the Chinese desire to raise its economy's stature at the expense of the US economy. The facts that the US is no longer the Saudis' Number One oil customer, and that the Saudis are already selling a great quantity of their oil to China makes their support for the renminbi as a reserve currency far more likely than it was only a few years ago.

---

[76] http://www.breitbart.com/Big-Peace/2013/10/17/Why-China-Wants-to-Dump-the-Dollar

[77] Id.

In fact, the Saudis have—since at least 2012—been saying that the world needs more "diversity" in reserve currencies and that it is "unnatural" that the renminbi isn't a major participant in the foreign exchange market.[78]

Whether or not the Saudis' motivation for a move to the renminbi is purely economic, it means that while the United States still has a major economic and national security interest in Saudi Arabia, the Saudis' interest in the U.S. is diminishing.

Nevertheless, the U.S., for the foreseeable future, will be a defender of the Saudis' national security at least with respect to overt foreign aggression—with China waiting in the wings should the relationship continue to deteriorate.

The Iranians' ability to cause a confluence of threats leading to significant crisis in Saudi Arabia is sufficient for us to gauge Saudi Arabia's stability worthy of a "YELLOW LIGHT" warning. If we are measuring Saudis' instability by estimating the likelihood of a crisis in the next three to five years, we have to conclude that there is a 65% likelihood of a regime-destabilizing crisis in that time.

Conclusion

Because of its wealth, its size, its significance to Islam and its relative stability, Saudi Arabia is the leader of the Sunni vanguard. The fact that it is divorcing itself from President Obama's foreign policy—and from the prominence a Security Council seat would have given it in the United Nations—means that its foreign policies will be decided internally and in consultation with other Sunni Muslim powers, not with the West.

The March 2011 joint military operation by the Saudis and the UAE to invade Bahrain in opposition to Shia forces there is of enormous significance. That action was uncharacteristic for a nation that was content to rely on the protection of America's nuclear umbrella and the U.S. ability to project power in the Middle East; it meant that Saudi Arabia had,

---

78 http://articles.chicagotribune.com/2012-05-22/news/sns-rt-saudi-econmin-interviewl5e8gmcm6-20120522_1_chinese-yuan-saudi-arabia-reserves

for the first time in memory, chosen to go it alone and confront the most dangerous power in its region.

But it did so in the interest of stability, which must not be confused with peace or democracy. The Saudis, and the Sunni vanguard they lead, are interested only in stabilizing the regimes that make up the vanguard. For the next three to five years—or at least until the Obama administration ends its term in office—any confluence of policy between our government and the Saudis' will be purely coincidental.

ARAB SPRING, EGYPT'S WINTER

DAVID P. GOLDMAN

THE SO-CALLED ARAB SPRING in Egypt began in January 2011 with the overthrow of Hosni Mubarak, an American ally of thirty years' standing, and ended in November with the restoration of the country's cold-war alliance with Russia. America's determination to depose Mubarak's military-backed regime and to lead the most populous Arab country towards democracy had nearly unanimous bi-partisan support, with the Obama administration vying with the Republican mainstream in its zeal to sweep out the old regime erred and foster a Western-style democracy. The drive for a new democratic Egypt was buoyed by a wave of popular sentiment, and serenaded by rapturous media accounts of young, hip revolutionaries toppling a sclerotic dictatorship.

Instead of moving forward to a new era of democracy, Egypt set the clock back to 1973, before then President Anwar Sadat expelled Russian advisors and prepared the way for an alliance with the United States.

Egypt's political crisis stemmed from external economic shocks. It faces no external threats, and only minor and ultimately managable internal threats from Islamic radicals including elements of al-Qaeda. Although Egypt fought three wars with Israel from 1947 through 1973, a cold peace with the Jewish state has held firm for nearly four decades, and there is no conceivable scenario under which Jerusalem would seek conflict with Cairo. The radical Hamas government in Gaza represents a prospective haven for terrorists and a source of weapons, but the Egyptian military has shown itself fully capable of controlling its common border with the Palestinian rump state. Although the use of Nile water is the source of a running dispute with Ethiopia, it is far below the level of a prospective casus belli. Egypt's neighbors (Libya, Sudan) are too weak to engage Egypt militarily. Egypt's military budget is several times the combined spending of its neighbors excluding Israel, and its air force flies 216 F-16s.

Egypt and its Neighbors: Armed Forces Comparison

	Personnel	Budget
Egypt	468,500	$28 billion
Sudan	109,300	$4 billion
Ethiopia	182,500	$0.4 billion
Libya	35,000	NA

Egypt is a unique, standalone case of a country unburdened by external threats and comfortable in its alliances (with the United States and the Sunni Arab world) whose civic life was undermined by the consequences of economic backwardness in a changing world economy. Its military exists less to defend the country than to impose social order from the top.

It is a banana republic without the bananas. Once the breadbasket of the Mediterranean, it imports half its caloric consumption. It ranks 118th among the world's nations in Transparency International's Corruption Perceptions Index. After sixty-two years in power, the country's military rulers own 30% of its economy. Most of the country remains locked in the premodern world of traditional society characterized by illiteracy, genital mutilation and consanguineous marriages. It is a horrible example of how socialism and cultural backwardness can push an economy past the point of no return, such that no policy remedy can reverse the deterioration through the actions of domestic economic factors. The country came to the brink of starvation during the first months of 2013 and survives as of this writing on a subsidy from Arab oil states of about $15 billion a year.

Because Egypt's economic problems are so intractable the likelihood is that the crisis will deepen over time. Egypt's military will succeed in crushing the Muslim Brotherhood as an organized force, but elements of the Brotherhood as well as overtly terrorist organizations will remain active and seek opportunity to destabilize the military government. Egypt's allies among Sunni states in the Persian Gulf will maintain an economic subsidy sufficient to avert outright starvation for the time being, because the Sunni states seek unity against the threat posed by Iran and its Shi'ite allies in Syria and Lebanon. Such a subsidy cannot last forever, and Egypt's medium-term prospects for stability are poor.

American policy ignored the facts on the Egyptian ground. Among the world's larger countries, Egypt is among the least prepared to compete in the modern world. Half of Egyptians live on $2 a day or less, and nearly half of them are functionally illiterate. According to a World Health Organization study, 97 percent of Egypt's married women have suffered genital mutilation, and 70 percent stated their intention to arrange the similar mutilation of their daughters, even though the Egyptian government outlawed the practice in 2007. Almost a third of Egyptians marry first or second cousins, the fail-safe indicator of a clan-based society. Only half of the 51 million Egyptians between the ages of 15 and 64 are counted in the government's measure of the labor force, which is why the official unemployment rate stands at only 11%. America's labor force of 153 million, by contrast, comprises three-quarters of the population aged 15 to 64. If Egypt's labor force were counted in the same way as America's, the unemployment rate would be 40%. The effective unemployment rate is even higher, for three-fifths of Egyptians live off the land, while the country imports half its caloric consumption. Agriculture productivity in Egypt is so poor that most farm labor must be considered disguised unemployment. Local wheat yields are only 18 bushels per acre, compared to 30 to 60 for non-irrigated wheat in the United States, and up 100 bushels for irrigated land. 30% of Egyptians of the relevant age, moreover, attend university, while only half graduate, and of those, few find employment.

Perhaps an additional 3 million Egyptian unemployed are warehoused in the university system. "Many people have degrees but they do not have the skill set," Masood Ahmed, director of the Middle East and Asia department of the International Monetary Fund said in a Jan. 29, 2011 Associated Press interview. "The scarce resource is talent," agreed Omar Alghanim, a prominent Gulf businessman. The employment pool available in the region "is not at all what's needed in the global economy." Samir Radwan, who briefly served as Egypt's finance minister after the February 2011 revolution, told the *Financial Times* Feb 13, 2011, "I'm generalizing, but a large number of the Egyptian labor force is unemployable. The products of the education system are unemployable." Egypt's workforce consists of a mass of unproductive peasants capped by a thin layer of unemployable graduates of state-run diploma mills. There are many highly-qualified Egyptian professionals, but most of them (like the Muslim Brotherhood's Morsi, an American-trained civil engineer) are educated overseas and, like Wael Ghonim, work overseas.

Wheat (US Dollars per Bushel)

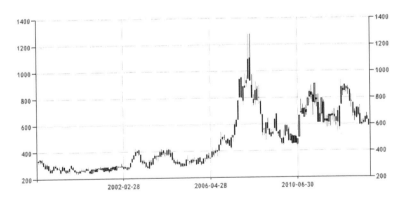

SOURCE: *TRADING ECONOMICS*

The trigger for the collapse of the Mubarak regime in January 2011 was an event as mundane as the spike in wheat prices to $9 a bushel. Political instability in response to the main source of calories for most

Egyptians was foreseeable well in advance, and some economists warned of the crackup to come. Reinhard Cluse of Union bank of Switzerland told the *Financial Times* August 6, 2010:

> Significant hikes in the global price of wheat would present the government with a difficult dilemma. Do they want to pass on price rises to end consumers, which would reduce Egyptians' purchasing power and might lead to social discontent? Or do they keep their regulation of prices tight and end up paying higher subsidies for food? In which case the problem would not go away but end up in the government budget. Egypt's public debt is already high, at roughly 74% of gross domestic product (GDP), according to UBS. Earlier this year the IMF projected that Egypt's food subsidies would cost the equivalent of 1.1% of GDP in 2009–10, while subsidies for energy were expected to add up to 5.1%. Tensions over food have led to violence in bread queues before and it wouldn't take much of a price rise for the squeeze on many consumers to become unbearably tight.

With the 2007 spike in wheat prices, Egypt's inflation rate tripled, from low single digits in the early 2000's to double-digits after 2007. By 2010 food price inflation had jumped to 18.5%. The *Financial Times* quoted economist Angus Blair on August 30, 2010: "You have to look at food price inflation in Egypt, which is the highest of any country in the

Egypt Inflation Rate
Annual Change on Consumer Price Index

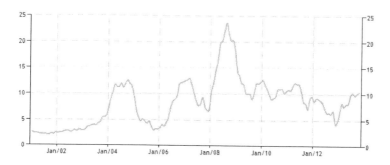

world at 18.5 per cent year on year. When a big chunk of society earns only a few dollars a day, this kind of food inflation is unsustainable."

The world wheat supply dropped by only 2.4% between 2009 and 2010—and the wheat price doubled. That's because affluent Asians don't care what they pay for grain. In econo-speak, grain is price inelastic: even a very large price increase won't reduce demand.

Before he went to Tahrir Square and discovered Wael Ghonim, the *Times'* Thomas Friedman wrote on February 5, 2011:

> Of course, China per se is not fueling the revolt here—but China and the whole Asian-led developing world's rising consumption of meat, corn, sugar, wheat and oil certainly is. The rise in food and gasoline prices that slammed into this region in the last six months clearly sharpened discontent with the illegitimate regimes—particularly among the young, poor and unemployed.

The trouble is that Chinese pigs will eat before the Egyptian poor.

Shifting Alliances

At the nadir of the country's economic fortunes, Egypt's military regained control in July 2013, and, spurned by Washington, revived the old alliance with Russia. Speaking to the visitiing Russian Foreign Minister Sergei Lavrov at a Nov. 14 press conference in Cairo, Egypt's foreign minister Nabil Fahmy declared: "We want to give a new impetus to our relations and return them to the same high level that used to exist with the Soviet Union." Responded Lavrov: ""We respect Egypt's sovereignty and the right of the Egyptians to decide on their fate. We expect that current efforts, including the development of a new constitution and a referendum on this basic law to make further progress and achieve the goals set by Egypt." Egypt reportedly will buy $2 billion of advanced weapons from Russia. Most remarkable of all is that Egypt's arms package with Russia will be financed by Saudi Arabia, another disillusioned American ally.

It is hard to find a parallel in the postwar period for a foreign policy initiative embraced so universally and with such enthusiasm. It is also hard to think of a policy failure so swift, complete and abject. Egypt was a centerpiece of American foreign policy since the Carter Administration. Originally, President Obama saw Egypt as America's bridge to the Muslim world. In July 2009 he delivered his address to Muslims from the cathedra of Cairo's leading Islamic institution, al-Azhar University, declaring, "I have come here to seek a new beginning between the United States and Muslims around the world; one based upon mutual interest and mutual respect; and one based upon the truth that America and Islam are not exclusive, and need not be in competition."

In February 2011, after three weeks of anti-regime demonstrations, President Obama demanded President Mubarak's resignation in a televised address:

> The Egyptian people have been told that there was a transition of authority, but it is not yet clear that this transition is immediate, meaningful or sufficient. The Egyptian government must put forward a credible, concrete and unequivocal path toward genuine democracy, and they have not yet seized that opportunity... We therefore urge the Egyptian government to move swiftly to explain the changes that have been made, and to spell out in clear and unambiguous language the step-by-step process that will lead to democracy and the representative government that the Egyptian people seek.... There must be restraint by all parties. Violence must be forsaken. It is imperative that the government not respond to the aspirations of their people with repression or brutality. The voices of the Egyptian people must be heard.

Only two years later Obama lost interest in Egypt, as his National Security Adviser Susan Rice told the *New York Times* Oct. 26, 2013. "Everything in the Middle East [but Iran and the Israel-Palestinian issue] would take a back seat," the *Times* reported. "That includes Egypt, which was once a central pillar of American foreign policy. Mr. Obama, who hailed the crowds on the streets of Cairo in 2011 and pledged to heed the cries for change across the region, made clear that there were limits to what the United States would do to nurture democracy, whether there, or in Bahrain, Libya, Tunisia or Yemen."

The fall of Muburak in February 2011 led to the victory of the Muslim Brotherhood, the only well-organized opposition party, in parliamentary elections held between November 2011 and February 2012. Presidential elections in June 2012 brought Muslim Brotherhood leader Mohammed Morsi to power and the Brotherhood proceeded to impose an Islamist constitution on Egypt, prompting the withdrawal of liberal and Christian parties from the constitutional assembly in November 2012. Morsi then demanded rule by decree, eliminating judicial review of presidential decisions. In an election marred by low turnout and large protests, Egyptian voters approved Morsi's constitution in December 2012. But Morsi's victory was Pyrrhic: food and energy shortages became acute and the Egyptian currency began to slide as Egypt's central bank ran out of reserves and the ability to borrow. By late June of 2013, protests against Morsi built up into a 30-million-person rally across Egypt. On July 3, Egypt's military removed Morsi from power with overwhelming popular support.

After eight-four years in opposition, the Muslim Brotherhood came to power, and burnt out like a penny sparkler. As this book goes to press, Mohammed Morsi is on trial in Cairo among fourteen other Muslim Brotherhood leaders for incitement to murder. Warnings that the trial of Egypt's former leader and first elected president would lead to violent protests turned out to be hollow. Youssef Hamza wrote in *The National* (United Arab Emirates) Nov. 23, 2013, "From street protests and condemnation by foreign and domestic human-rights groups to a rousing speech by the deposed Islamist president that would ignite the streets. It never happened. Instead, the appearance of Mohammed Morsi in court this month proved to be a public-relations victory for the military-backed government... The Anti-Coup Alliance, an umbrella organisation of Islamists, had called for massive protests on the first day of the trial. However, only small pockets of people turned out, lending legitimacy to the interim government."

American policy on both wings of the political spectrum proceeded from faulty perceptions.

1. America mistook a popular reaction to impending economic breakdown for a forward-looking movement for modernization. Egypt's

2011 crisis had its origins in the Arab nation's inabiity to adapt to the changing global economy. The country stood on the verge of economic freefall before the so-called Arab Spring erupted in Tunisia, and the political chaos that ensued upon Mubarak's February 2011 overthrow send the country's fragile economy into virtual shutdown.

2. America assumed that the forms of parliamentary demoracy would moderate the Islamist opposition to to Egypt's military government, the Muslim Brotherhood. The Muslim Brotherhood melds Islamist ideology with the organization discipline of a modern totalitarian political party, and its antipathy to Western interests is bred in the bone.

3. America assumed that the young activists who occupied Tahrir Square in January 2011 and exchanged signals via social media embodied the ideals of a new generation of Egyptians that resonated with Western values.

4. The American public fell in love with the young democracy activists who floated across the surface of the Arab revolts like benzene bubbles on the Nile. More precisely, Americans fell in love with their own image, in the persons of hip young Egyptians who reminded them of Americans. Henry Kissinger harrumphed that the Tahrir Square activists could not rule Egypt because they represented no constituency, but no-one was listening.

Thomas Friedman, the bellwether of conventional wisdom in American journalism, wrote on Feb. 11, 2011, just before Mubarak's downfall:

The Tahrir Square uprising "has nothing to do with left or right," said Dina Shehata, a researcher at Al-Ahram Center for Political and Strategic Studies. "It is about young people rebelling against a regime that has stifled all channels for their upward mobility. They want to shape their own destiny, and they want social justice" from a system in which a few people have gotten fantastically rich, in giant villas, and everyone else has stagnated. Any ideological group that tries to hijack these young people today will lose.

One of the best insights into what is happening here is provided by a 2009 book called "Generation in Waiting," edited by Navtej Dhillon and Tarik Yousef, which examined how young people are coming of age in eight Arab countries. It contends that the great game that is unfolding in the Arab world today is not related to political Islam but is a "generational game" in which more than 100 million young Arabs are pressing against stifling economic and political structures that have stripped all their freedoms and given them in return one of the poorest education systems in the world, highest unemployment rates and biggest income gaps.

"It is no surprise," Friedman added, "that the emerging spokesman for this uprising is Wael Ghonim—a Google marketing executive who is Egyptian." Conservatives and liberals were competing to lionize Google sales manager Wael Ghonim. Caroline Kennedy gave him the JFK Profiles in Courage Award in May 2011. He made *Time Magazine*'s list of the world's 100 most influential people and kicked off the magazine's annual gala that year. The magazine Arabian Business pegged him as the second most powerful Arab in the world.

Conservatives were not to be outdone by the liberal enthusiasm for hip Egyptian democracy. The conservative Lebanese scholar Fouad Ajami gushed in the *Wall Street Journal* of Feb. 12, 2011, "No turbaned ayatollah had stepped forth to summon the crowd. This was not Iran in 1979. A young Google executive, Wael Ghonim, had energized this protest when it might have lost heart, when it could have succumbed to the belief that this regime and its leader were a big, immovable object. Mr. Ghonim was a man of the modern world. He was not driven by piety. The condition of his country—the abject poverty, the crony economy of plunder and corruption, the cruelties and slights handed out to Egyptians in all walks of life by a police state that the people had outgrown and despaired of—had given this young man and others like him their historical warrant."

At the conservative *Weekly Standard*, Elliot Abrams, a former official on the Bush National Security Council, was more direct in demanding Mubarak's departure in a Feb. 11 post: "Not a single significant step toward democracy was taken during all those years of quiet… Under [Mubarak], Egypt's prestige and influence in the Arab League and throughout the region have declined to an historic low. To hang on these extra months he has thrust the country into chaos. The longer it continues the harder it will be for Egypt to find a path to real democracy."

"Fears of a Muslim Brotherhood takeover are overblown" read the headline of the next item on the Weekly Standard website Feb. 11. Ali Alyami wrote, "The chance that Islamists will capture the Arab uprisings is slim unless anti-democratic, oil rich Arab dynasties like the Saudi and other Gulf monarchs, or their Iranian rivals, are allowed to pour billions of dollars into the coffers of their respective proxies."

That day Mubarak stepped down, and Obama took to television to exult: "Egyptians have made it clear that nothing less than genuine democracy will carry the day… It was the moral force of nonviolence— not terrorism and mindless killing—that bent the arc of history toward justice once more." By May the Muslim Brotherhood was in power, not with the support of the Gulf monarchies, but despite their bitter objections.

Not since the Kosovo war of 1998 was American opinion as unanimous as in enthusiasm for the so-called Arab Spring during first months of 2011. Republicans vied with the Obama administration in their zeal for the ouster of Egypt's dictator Hosni Mubarak and the subsequent NATO intervention against the Qaddafi government in Libya. Rousing cheers drowned out the few voices of dissent. The Obama administration saw its actions as a proof that soft power in pursuit of humanitarian goals offered a new foreign policy paradigm. And the Republican establishment saw a vindication of the Bush freedom agenda. Both were wrong.

"Revolutions are sweeping the Middle East and everyone is a convert to George W. Bush's freedom agenda," Charles Krauthammer observed in February 2011. "Now that revolution has spread from Tunisia to Oman," Krauthammer added, "the [Obama] administration is rushing to keep up with the new dispensation, repeating the fundamental tenet of the Bush Doctrine that Arabs are no exception to the universal thirst for dignity and freedom." And William Kristol exulted, "Helping the Arab

Spring through to fruition might contribute to an American Spring, one of renewed pride in our country and confidence in the cause of liberty."

Just two years later, the foreign policy establishment has fractured in the face of a Syrian civil war that threatens to metastasize into neighboring Iraq and Lebanon, and an Egyptian economic collapse that has brought the largest Arab country to the brink of state failure. Some Republican leaders, including Sen. John McCain and *Weekly Standard* editor William Kristol, demand American military intervention to support Syria's Sunni rebels. But Daniel Pipes, the dean of conservative Middle East analysts, wrote April 11 that "Western governments should support the malign dictatorship of Bashar al-Assad," because "Western powers should guide enemies to stalemate by helping whichever side is losing, so as to prolong their conflict." And the respected strategist Edward Luttwak contends that America should "leave bad enough alone" in Syria and turn its attention away from the Middle East, to Asia. The Obama administration meanwhile is waffling about what might constitute a "red line" for intervention and what form such intervention might take.

The former consensus has shrunk to the common observation that all the available choices are bad. It could get much worse. Western efforts have failed to foster a unified leadership among the Syrian rebels, and jihadi extremists appear in control of the Free Syrian Army. Syria's war is "creating the conditions for a renewed conflict, dangerous and complex, to explode in Iraq. If Iraq is not shielded rapidly and properly, it will definitely slip into the Syrian quagmire," warns Arab League Ambassador Nassif Hitti, and Iraq leaders are talking of civil war and eventual partition. Hezbollah chief Hassan Nasrallah, meanwhile, warned May 1, "Syria has real friends in the region, and the world will not let Syria fall into the hands of America, Israel or takfiri [radical islamist] groups," threatening in effect to turn the civil war into a regional conflict. The Syrian conflict has the potential to destabilize Turkey. And the gravest risk to the region remains the likelihood that "inherent weaknesses of state and society in Egypt reach a point where the country's political, social and economic systems no longer function," as Gamal Abuel Hassan wrote May 28.

This is a tragic outcome, in the strict sense of the term, for it is hard to imagine how it could have turned out otherwise. In January

2012, after the first hopes for Arab democracy had faded, former Bush administration official Elliot Abrams insisted, "The neocons, democrats, and others who applauded the Arab uprisings were right, for what was the alternative? To applaud continued oppression? To instruct the rulers on better tactics, the way Iran is presumably lecturing (and arming) Syria's Bashar al-Assad? Such a stance would have made a mockery of American ideals, would have failed to keep these hated regimes in place for very long, and would have left behind a deep, almost ineradicable anti-Americanism." The neoconservatives mistook a tubercular fever for the flush of youth in the Arab revolts, to be sure, but they read the national mood aright, just as did the Obama administration.

The Republican hawks advocated the furtherance of the Arab Spring by force of arms, starting with Libya. On Feb. 25, 2011, a month after Mubarak's fall, William Kristol's Foreign Policy Initiative garnered forty-five signatures of past officials and public intellectuals "urging President Obama, in conjunction with NATO allies, to take action to end the violence being propagated by the regime of Muammar al-Qaddafi." Three weeks later a NATO force led by the United States intervened. By September, the Qaddafi regime was beaten, and Robert Kagan lauded President Obama in The Weekly Standard: "By intervening, with force, the NATO alliance not only saved the people of Libya and kept alive the momentum of the Arab Spring...the end of Qaddafi's rule is a great accomplishment for the Obama administration and for the president personally. Furthermore, the president deserves credit because his decision was unpopular and politically risky." A month later the victorious rebels put the cadavers of Qaddafi and his son on public view for four days.

The national consensus behind the Arab Spring peaked with the Libyan venture. Elliot Abrams was in a sense right: to intimate that democracy might not apply to Arabs seems to violate America's first principle, that people of all background have the same opportunity for success—in the United States. It seems un-American to think differently. Isn't America a multi-ethnic melting pot where all religions and ethnicities have learned to get along? That is a fallacy of composition, to be sure: Americans are brands plucked out of the fire of failed cultures, the few who fled the tragic failings of their own culture to make a fresh start. America is girded by a figurative River Jordan, in which wanderers wash away the original sin of ethnic origin. The only tragic thing about America is the incapacity of Americans to comprehend the tragedy of other peoples. To pronounce judgment on other cultures as unfit for modernity, as Abrams wrote, seems "a mockery of American ideals." The trouble is that America can make Americans out of immigrants from any corner of the world, but it cannot export its own character. It is a widespread misimpression (and one reinforced by conspiracy theorists seeking the malign influence of the "Israel Lobby") that the neoconservative movement is in some way Jewish thing. On the contrary, it is a distinctly American thing. As the born-again Methodist George W. Bush said in 2003, "Peoples of the Middle East share a high civilization, a religion of personal responsibility, and a need for freedom as deep as our own. It is not realism to suppose that one-fifth of humanity is unsuited to liberty; it is pessimism and condescension, and we should have none of it." The Catholic neoconservative and natural-law theorist Michael Novak put it just as passionately in his 2004 book *The Universal Hunger for Liberty*: "The hunger for liberty has only slowly been felt among Muslims. That hunger is universal, even when it is latent, for the preconditions for it slumber in every human breast." Novak praised the "hopeful majority of Muslims [who] refuse to concede that Islam is incompatible with universal human rights, personal dignity, and opportunity."

By contrast, Israelis were overwhelmingly pessimistic about the outcome of the Arab revolts, and aghast at the celerity with which Washington dumped Mubarak. "The message to the Middle East is that it doesn't pay to be an American ally," a former Israeli intelligence chief told me in 2012. Although the prominent Soviet refusenik turned Israeli politician, Nathan Sharansky, believed in a universal desire for democracy, the vast majority of Israeli opinion thought the idea mad. As Joshua Muravchik wrote in 2011, the Arab Spring "precipitated a sharp split between neoconservatives and hard-headed Israeli analysts who had long been their allies and friends. While neocons saw democratization as a balm to soothe the fevered brow of the Arab world, Israeli strategists (with the notable exception of Natan Sharansky) thought this utterly naive. Their message in essence was this: you do not know the Arabs as we do. Difficult as their governments are to deal with, they are more reasonable than their populations. Democratization of the Arab world would lead to radicalization, which would be a bane to you and us."

The Israelis are accustomed to living with long-term uncertainty; Americans want movies with happy endings. The alternative to the Bush Freedom Agenda or Obama's proposed reconciliation with the Muslim world would have been ugly: the strategic equivalent of a controlled burn in a forest fire, as Daniel Pipes proposed: prolonging conflict, at frightful human cost, as the Reagan administration did during the Iran–Iraq War of the 1980s. It was one thing to entice prospective enemies into a war of attrition in the dark corners of the Cold War, though, and quite another to do so under the klieg lights. The strategy might have been correct on paper, but Americans are not typically in the market for pessimism.

The neoconservatives triumphantly tracked the progress of what they imagined was Arab democracy. Max Boot wrote after Iraq's March 2005 elections, "In 2003, more than a month before the invasion of Iraq, I wrote in the Weekly Standard that the forthcoming fall of Baghdad 'may turn out to be one of those hinge moments in history—events like the storming of the Bastille or the fall of the Berlin Wall—after which everything is different. If the occupation goes well (admittedly a big if), it may mark the moment when the powerful antibiotic known as democracy was introduced into the diseased environment of the Middle East, and began to transform the region for the better.' Well, who's the simpleton now? Those who dreamed of spreading democracy to the Arabs or those who denied that it could ever happen?"

And in April 2011, William Kristol wrote in *The Weekly Standard*, "The Arab winter is over. The men and women of the Greater Middle East are no longer satisfied by 'a little life.' Now it's of course possible that this will turn out to be a false spring. But surely it's not beyond the capacity of the United States and its allies to help reformers in the Arab world achieve mostly successful outcomes....Here, early in the twenty-first century, the Arabs seem to be rising to the occasion. The question is, will we?.... And who knows? Helping the Arab Spring through to fruition might contribute to an American Spring, one of renewed pride in our country and confidence in the cause of liberty."

Kissinger published an I-told-you-so in August 2012: "The United States applauded the demonstrations in Egypt's Tahrir Square. Blaming itself for too protracted an association with an undemocratic leader, it urged Hosni Mubarak to step down. But once he did so, the original exultant demonstrators have not turned out to be the heirs. Instead, Islamists with no record of democracy and a history of hostility to the West have been elected to a presidency they had pledged not to seek."

By 2012, young Mr. Ghonim had disappeared from public view. He was last sighted on June 25, 2013, in an Internet video asking the Muslim Brotherhood president Mohammed Morsi to step down. On July 1, thirty million Egyptians—more than a third of the country's total population took to the streets to demand Morsi's ouster and a return of military rule in the name of national salvation.

For a few months the Egyptian rebellion captivated Americans because people like Wael Ghonim affirm our self-admiration. Now that Mr. Ghonim no longer is trending, the media has moved on and the public has lost interest. In reality, Egypt's story is dreary and depressing. Sixty years of socialism commencing with Gamel Abdul Nasser's 1952 military takeover left the Egyptian economy so backward that it is incapable of feeding itself, much less offering its people the hope of economic advancement. It cannot modernize its economy because its population is too backward to take on the task of modernization.

Harder to explain in retrospect is the fact that both the Obama administration and the Republican mainstream staked its reputation on the Muslim Brotherhood as an agent of democratic transformation. The Obama administration had backed the Muslim Brotherhood from the beginning to the end of the crisis, with catastrophic results for American influence in the region. On Feb. 10, 2011, the day before Mubarak resigned, Obama's Direction of National Intelligence James Clapper told a Congressional hearing: "The term Muslim Brotherhood is an umbrella term for a variety of movements. In the case of Egypt, a very heterogeneous group, largely secular, which has eschewed violence and has decried al-Qaeda as a perversion of Islam." Clapper's statement was egregiously false: the Brotherhood was founded in 1928 by Hassan al-Banna as a vanguard party dedicated to restoring Islamic rule throughout the region, and guided during its formative years by the fundamentalist firebrand Sayyid Qutb, hanged in 1966 for plotting the assassination of then Presidnet Gamal Abdel Nasser. Clapper's press spokesman demurred that the intelligence direction "is well aware that the Muslim Brotherhood is not a seuclar organization," but the Obama administration backed it nonetheless.

On April 3, 2012, between the parliamentary and presidential elections that put Mohammed Morsi into power, the *Washington Post* reported, "Members of Egypt's Muslim Brotherhood began a week-long charm offensive in Washington on Tuesday, meeting with White House officials, policy experts and others to counter persistent fears about the group's emergence as the country's most powerful political force." After meetings at the White House, Obama's spokesman Jay Carney announced, "The Muslim Brotherhood will play a prominent role in Egypt's life going forward."

If anything, the Republican mainstream evinced more enthusiasm for the Muslim Brotherhood than the administration. Reuel Marc Gerecht, a fellow at the Foundation for Defense of Democracies and a frequent contributor to *The Weekly Standard*, opined in the *Wall Street Journal* on April 23, 2012:

> What is poorly understood in the West is how critical fundamentalists are to the moral and political rejuvenation of their countries. As counterintuitive as it seems, they are the key to more democratic, liberal politics in the region…We can easily find truly disturbing commentary and actions by members of the Egyptian Brotherhood, or by the Tunisian Rachid Ghannouchi, the intellectual guru behind the ruling Nahda Party. But we can just as easily find words and deeds that ought to make us consider the possibility that these men are neither Ernest Röhm and his fascist Brownshirts nor even religious versions of secular autocrats. Rather, they are cultural hybrids trying to figure out how to combine the best of the West (material progress and the absence of brutality in daily life) without betraying their faith and pride.

Mainstream Republicans remained true believers in the healing power of democracy throughout the Egyptian crisis. Ideologues like Gerecht advised the Republicans to ignore the ugly face of Islamism and look to the inevitable triumph of democratic institutions. As Gerecht wrote in the *Wall Street Journal*:

> As is already happening in Egypt, we will see debates revolving around issues that will turn Western stomachs—such as the exclusion of Christians and women from official positions, and the permissibility of clitoridectomy and childhood brides....But democracy, even if vastly more limited than current Western practice, always introduces a jousting ethic into politics. Representative government puts into play the sacred and the profane. It empowers women, the Achilles' heel of Islamic fundamentalism. In Egypt, it pits Muslim Brothers against more hard-core Salafists. Secular Muslim liberals may one day form a government. But for now, they are too culturally close to the West, and to the Westernized dictators, to carry their societies with them.

As Egypt's economy and political system went into free-fall during 2012 and 2013, the American foreign policy establishment clung to its belief that the mere form of parliamentary democracy would overcome all problems. By the time that the Egyptian military stepped in to pick up the pieces, American influence in Egypt was virtually extinguished.

A week after Mubarak's overthrow, the Muslim Brotherhood's spiritual leader Sheikh Yusuf al-Qaradawi returned to Egypt after three decades of exile in Qatar, whose former Emir sponsored the Brotherhood along with vanity projects like al-Jazeera Television. As the *New York Times* wrote Feb. 18, 2011, "An intellectual inspiration to the outlawed Muslim Brotherhood, Sheik Qaradawi was jailed in Egypt three times for his ties to the group and spent most of his life abroad. His prominence exemplifies the peril and potential for the West as Egypt opens up. While he condemned the 9/11 attacks, he has supported suicide bombers against Israel and attacks on American forces in Iraq." Speaking to an audience of millions in Tahrir Square, Qaradawi called for Egyptian revolution and Muslim conquest of Jerusalem.

The Brotherhood's embrace of Qaradawi immediately after the military government's fall should have been a warning to the West. Throughout his career he supported not only violent jihad including suicide attacks, but the most barbaric practices of Egyptian traditional society, for example

female genital mutilation. In a fatwa published on the website IslamOn-
line, Qaradawi wrote:

> The most moderate opinion and the most likely one to be correct
> is in favor of practicing circumcision in the moderate Islamic way
> indicated in some of the Prophet's hadiths—even though such
> hadiths are not confirmed to be authentic. It is reported that the
> Prophet (peace and blessings be upon him) said to a midwife:
> "Reduce the size of the clitoris but do not exceed the limit, for that
> is better for her health and is preferred by husbands."

The notion that a modern democracy can be built in a country that
subjects the overwhelming majority of women to physical mutilation is
one of the strangest ever to afflict Western political scientists.

Among the first actions of the newly-elected Muslim Brotherhood
government was to crush the liberal activists who had captured the
American imagination in Tahrir square a year earlier. A network of
American non-governmental organizations (NGO's) had trained and
supported the democracy activists before and after Mubarak's resignation. In February 2012, the Morsi government put sixteen Americans on trial for allegedly accepting illegal foreign funding to interfere
in Egyptian politics. Among them was the son of Ray LaHood, then
Obama's Secretary of Transportation. This failed to shake the faith of
Republican leaders in the Muslim Brotherhood as an instrument of
Arab democracy. Sen. Lindsey Graham (R.–NC) met with Brotherhood
leaders and pronounced them worthy of American partnership. Matt
Bradley reported in the *Wall Street Journal* Feb. 21, 2012:

> After talking with the Muslim Brotherhood, I was struck with their
> commitment to change the law because they believe it's unfair,"
> said Sen. Lindsey Graham (R., S.C.), who was traveling with Mr.
> McCain. Mr. Graham and other lawmakers praised the Brother-
> hood, whose Freedom and Justice Party won a plurality of nearly
> 50% of the seats in Parliament, as a strong potential partner for
> the future of U.S. relations with Egypt.
>
> That marks a dramatic change from several months ago, when
> some Republican politicians reacted warily to the Brotherhood's

rising clout. In April 2011, Mr. Graham said he was suspicious of the Brotherhood's "agenda," and that "their motives are very much in question."

"I was very apprehensive when I heard the election results," Mr. Graham said on Monday. "But after visiting and talking with the Muslim Brotherhood I am hopeful that…we can have a relationship with Egypt where the Muslim Brotherhood is a strong political voice."

Neither the Obama administration nor the Republicans abandoned Morsi after his stance turned erratic and anti-American later in the year. On Sept. 11, 2012, Islamists assaulted the American embassy in Cairo in apparent coordination with the fatal attack on American diplomats in Cairo. It took President Mohamed Morsi two days to denounce the assault on the embassy, and even then he placed the blame on a hitherto unnoticed clip posted on YouTube rather than the attackers. For two days after the flag-burning, Egyptian security was absent while demonstrators threatened the embassy. "A single security vehicle was imaged making an occasional and completely feckless foray through the gathering area, during the early morning of 13 September in Cairo. No Egyptian police or military or other security personnel were present," the Nightwatch letter observed Sept. 13. The Muslim Brotherhood called for mass protests against the Youtube clip, albeit "peaceful" ones.

The White House said nothing when Morsi traveled to Iran in August 2012, breaking Iran's diplomatic isolation, believing (as the Council on Foreign Relations' Steven Cook put it) that Egypt would be a "more appropriate interlocutor" for Washington in the Middle East. And it offered an additional $1 billion of American aid, in the form of loan forgiveness and new credits, as well as backing for a $4.8 billion loan from the International Monetary Fund.

In January 2013, the media watchdog MEMRI discovered an Lebanese television interview in which Morsi claimed that peace negotiations between Israel and Palestinian Arabs were devised by "the Zionist and American enemies for the sole purpose of opposing the will of the Palestinian people…No reasonable person can expect any progress on this track." The Egyptian president added, "Either [you accept] the Zionists and everything they want, or else it is war. This is what these occupiers of the land of Palestine know—these blood-suckers, who attack the Palestinians, these warmongers, the descendants of apes and pigs." Egyptians should "nurse our children and grandchildren on hatred for Jews," he concluded. The ensuing scandal prompted the Obama administration to ask Morsi for a retraction, to which he responded that his statements were "taken out of context" and that he "does not accept...derogatory statements regarding any religion."

Sen. John McCain, the Republican presidential candidate in 2008, responded to the "apes and pigs" affair by calling on Egypt to sign an agreement with the International Monetary Fund to provide interim loans in return for sharp cuts in food and energy subsidies. In 2012, McCain had urged the administration to use aid to promote Egyptian democracy. But in January 2013 McCain called instead for American patience with the Morsi regime's missteps. "The fact is that the economy of Egypt is in such condition that it requires expeditious aid to be supplied," he said. "It is hard to have democracy when people are not eating." Senator Lindsey Graham, a Republican from South Carolina, urged Morsi to finalize the talks with the IMF to ease the flow of U.S. assistance. "The Egyptian economy is going to collapse if something is not done quickly," he said. "We urge the president, Morsi and he understands this, to get an agreement with the IMF." The IMF's cure, though appeared deadlier than the disease, and negotiations repeatedly failed.

The July 1, 2013 mass demonstration against the Muslim Brotherhood regime was the largest popular demonstration in world history. The number of Egyptians in the streets exceeded the total votes cast in the 2012 parliamentary elections (29.3 million), and vastly exceeded the votes cast for the Muslim Brotherhood. Yet the Obama Administration backed Morsi to the end. Many of the demonstrators carried signs denouncing President Obama for supporting "terrorism," namely the Muslim Brotherhood, and ridiculing US Ambassador to Egypt Anne Patterson as a "hazeboon," or old hag. Ambassador Patterson had urged Egypt's Coptic Christians not to participate in the coming demonstrations against the regime, and opposition activist Shady el-Ghazali alleged that Patterson had shown "blatant bias" in favor of Morsi and the Muslim Brotherhood.

Republicans for the most part agreed with the Obama administration. After Morsi's departure, Sen. McCain supported the Brotherhood's demand that the United States declare the shift a military coup and force a cutoff of American aid. "We met some Muslim Brotherhood representatives. They were senior-level people," McCain told The Daily Beast on Aug. 6, 2013. "They believe things are going to get a lot worse before they get better. They demand that [deposed President Mohamed] Morsi get released. They believe it was a military coup and they are very far apart from the military and the new government." By endorsing the Brotherhood's claim that its ouster constituted a "military coup," McCain in effect demanded the suspension of America's $1.3 billion annual military subsidy to Egypt. Two months later the Obama administration adopted the Republican position, and cut several hundred million dollars of aid to Egypt and suspended planned shipments of military aircraft and tanks.

Egypt percevies that it was abandoned not simply by one administration, but by both political parties and by the consensus of the American foreign policy establishment and major media. The collapse of the long-standing American-Egyptian alliance stemmed from a distorted vision of the problems of the Arab world across the American political spectrum.

* * *

The Muslim Brotherhood's ascent to power panicked Egypt's middle class and provoked capital flight that probably reduced the country's foreign exchange reserves by more than $15 billion. Like Russia during the first years after the collapse of Communism, capital left the country by every possible route, including smuggling of scarce fuel and food supplies notionally owned by the government. "In the Mediterranean town of Alexandria earlier this week," the Gazette reported on Sep. 27, 2013 "the military police seized 4.3 million liters of diesel hidden in stores ready for smuggling." While Egyptians faced 24-hour queues for diesel fuel at gasoline stations, tankers reportedly were waiting at Port Said on the Suez Canal to pump diesel oil from storage facilities. A black market in fertilizer has earned billions of dollars for senior officials, according to a Cairo University professor of agriculture quoted by the Egypt Gazette. The Gazette story alleges that Hosni Mubarak's agriculture minister Amin Abaza organized the fertilizer scam. Abaza at the time was awaiting trial on charges of illegally selling public land. Egyptian media also alleged that rice was vanishing from public storehouses, and that the government's food-distribution organization was peddling the contraband grain by the container on the overseas market.

The Nobel Laureate and presidential candidate Mohamed ElBaradei warned in September 2011 that Egypt would run out of foreign in exchange within six months. His estimate was off by a year, but in the right direction. The first fuel and food shortages appeared in the early spring of 2012. Fuel shortages have become critical in many parts of Egypt. According to the UN news service IRIN in an April 2, 2012 report from Cairo, "It has been three months since a fuel shortage hit Egypt, and people's patience is wearing thin amid fears the crisis could disrupt the production of subsidized bread. The government blames hoarding for the crisis. Thousands of cars queue outside petrol stations from early morning, while long queues form outside gas cylinder centers." More than a hundred Egyptian bakeries shut down in mid-April to protest the fuel shortage, the Egyptian news site Youm7. com reported April 12. In Beni Suef, dozens of bakery owners gathered in front of a government flour warehouse to complain that they could obtain fuel only at black market prices, which required them to sell bread at black market prices.

Western governments recognized the magnitude of the problem. Beset by their own financial problems, though, they were paralyzed. Meeting in May 2011 at Deauville, the Group of Eight industrial nations promised $20 to $40 billion in support for Egypt and Tunisia. The New York Times reported May 5, 2011, "The group's official communiqué promised $20 billion, which would be a major infusion of funds. President Nicolas Sarkozy of France, the meeting's host, said the total could be double that. But he and other officials did not specify how much each country and international development agency would provide, and the Group of 8 countries have in the past made commitments that they did not ultimately fulfill." Virtually none of the money materialized.

By the time that John McCain decided that the US should show "patience" for the Muslim Brotherhood's suppression of liberal activists, Egypt's economy was running on fumes and in acute danger of a food shortage. Public health clinics were out of vaccines for infants, importers were running out of stockpiles of basic food items, and the government owed $3 billion back payments to oil suppliers in the midst of a paralyzing fuel shortage. With cash on hand down to about $6 billion, or less than two months' imports, Egypt's central bank had no money to allocate to food importers. The country's importers association claimed that Egyptian firms cut imports in half since the January 2011 revolution, threatening essential food supplies. After the 2011 revolution, importers stocked up on food out of fear of devaluation. By the middle of 2012 they could not obtain credit to replace their diminishing supplies. Especially vulnerable is Egypt's provision of beans, the biggest staple after bread. High dollar prices and dwindling cash reverses could lead to a 40% reduction in the supply of imported foods, the importers warned in September 2012.

An Egyptian agreement with the International Monetary Fund was beyond the Morsi government's capacity to achieve. Egypt was running a budget deficit equal to about 15% of Gross Domestic Product, and nearly a third of that paid for fuel and food subsidies. Any attempt to cut subsidies, though, would have worsened critical shortages of essential items. Unable to reduce subsidies that account for most of a budget deficit that now exceeds 14 percent of GDP, and unwilling to raises taxes in the face of political opposition, President Morsi has taken the path of least resistance. Currency devaluation accomplishes the same thing as higher taxes or lower subsidies, that is, reducing consumption, but it does so in a haphazard way, by raising the price of imported items.

In September 2012, Egypt's leading daily Al-Ahram had reported that Upper Egypt was suffering a 30% shortage of diesel fuel. The newspaper wrote, "Egyptians started feeling another diesel crisis at the end of last week, with amounts available shrinking and prompting lengthy queues at stations. A shortage of liquidity in the Ministry of Petroleum has delayed payments to refineries that provide the crude needed to produce diesel. Egypt's fuel suppliers had stopped giving the country credit in late August. The London Independent commented Aug. 23,

2012 "The petrol shortage might detonate what analysts believe is a ticking time bomb involving the lavish fuel and food subsidies which the government uses to drive down prices for ordinary Egyptians. Hampered by piecemeal growth and reliant on high risk lenders, Mohamed Morsi may find it impossible to justify the decades-old subsidy system, which costs the government $16 billion a year and devours a fifth of the overall budget."

By the time it occurred to Sen. McCain in early 2013 that Egyptian democracy depended on a deal with the IMF, the patient was too weak to survive the operation that the Fund's economists recommended. While Sen. McCain urged "patience" for the Morsi regime, food protests erupted, Al-Ahram reported on Jan. 24, 2013:

On 25 and 28 January 2011, thousands chanted "Bread!" on streets across Egypt, highlighting the economic nature of the uprising. The chant represented the people's aspirations for a fairer economic system, protesting high inflation rates, low wages and the unavailability of daily rations. It is no coincidence that bread was the first word of the revolution's main slogan ("Bread, freedom, dignity"), as it is a daily staple for millions of people, making Egypt the largest per capita wheat consumer and importer.

"The demand for bread or daily rationing has been central to the Egyptian people's economic and social demands since the 1977 bread uprising," Khaled Ali, labour lawyer and ex-presidential candidate, told al-Ahram Online. "Food security is the Egyptians' most basic right and the people's struggle for enough to eat will continue," explained Ali.

It has been two years now, and matters seem to be deteriorating rather than stabilising. Food protests have continued after the revolution with inflation reaching new peaks and basic necessities moving further out of reach for whole communities.

The Obama administration asked Congress for an emergency $450 million cash infusion for Egypt in September 2012, but the Morsi government's hostile behavior during the assault on the American embassy earlier the same month ruled out Congressional approval. Representative Kay Granger of Texas, immediately announced that she would use her position as chairwoman of the House appropriations subcommittee overseeing foreign aid to block the distribution of the money. She said the American relationship with Egypt "has never been under more scrutiny" after the attack on the embassy.

Morsi meanwhile scrounged for support among his dwindling list of supporters in the Muslim world. Egypt announced that Turkey had promised $2 billion in aid, but Turkish press accounts explained that Egypt would not be able to spend any of that money. $1 billion is reserved to finance the operations of Turkish firms in Egypt, which did nothing for Egypt's urgent import requirements. The other $1 billion, the Turkish newspaper Star wrote on September 15, 2012, was just an advance on the prospective $4.8 billion loan from the International Monetary Fund (IMF). Turkey still owes the IMF $5 billion from its borrowing after the 2008 crisis, so it will expect repayment out of the IMF money. The IMF loan never came through so the money was never released.

By the spring of 2013, the Egyptian pound had fallen to just 60% of its 2012 exchange rate against the dollar, and the collapse of the currency translated directly into higher prices for beans, dairy products and meat. Before the military stepped in, food price inflation had priced everything but bread out of the reach of the poorer half of the population, and the bread supply was at risk.

Egypt was flat out of money. The central bank still claimed a few billion dollars of reserves, but the country owed $5 billion in arrears to companies that produce oil and gas on its territory. Half of the amount is overdue, and oil companies reportedly expect to wait years for payment. Egypt's arrears to on trade credits from suppliers of oil, wheat, and other essential items probably exceeded its $8.8 billion cash reserves. With a trade deficit running at $32 billion, Egypt was shutting off vital imports of food and energy.

Egypt's trade deficit exploded to a remarkable 15 percent of GDP, or $42 billion per year. Egypt's main foreign exchange earners apart from exports have been tourism, which peaked at $12 billion in 2010 and may fall to as little as $6 billion in 2013 by some Egyptian estimates, and the Suez Canal, which earns between $4 and $5 billion per year. Egyptians working abroad also send money home through remittances, which the

Egypt's Exports, Imports and Trade Balance

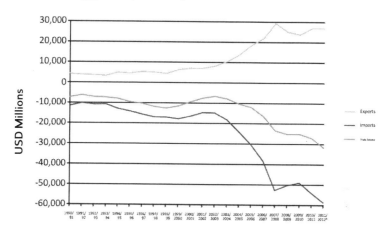

SOURCE: CENTRAL BANK OF EGYPT

World Bank estimated at $18 billion in 2010. It is impossible to know how much money Egyptians are sending home at the moment. Egypt has lost $20 billion in foreign exchange reserves since the fall of Hosni Mubarak in early 2011; how much of that reflects flight capital, and how much reflects financing of essential imports was impossible to judge.

The American foreign policy establishment nonetheless expected a rescue of Egypt's economy at the hands of Saudi Arabia, whose monarchy looks on the Muslim Brotherhood the way Captain Hook viewed the crocodile. The Brotherhood was founded to sweep away the old Arab monarchies and replace them with a modern form of Islamist governance based on twentieth-century totalitarian parties. Nonetheless the experts were confident that Saudi Arabia would ride to the rescue. Writing on August 2, 2012 in *The Tablet*, Fouad Ajami—who had written rapturously of Wael Ghonim a year earlier—decided that the Saudis were now Egypt's savior:

> In Egypt [Saudi Arabia] would find a natural partner. Egypt had taken time out from the game of nations: It had a revolution to settle, a fight for the makeup of a new order. With the triumph of the Muslim Brotherhood in the presidential election, the Egyptians were ready to return to the regional contest. Egypt is in desperate

Egypt Government Budget
Percentage of the GDP

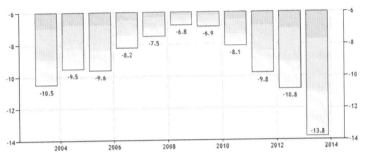

SOURCE: WWW.TRADINGECONOMICS.COM / MINISTRY OF FINANCE, EGYPT

Egypt Government Spending

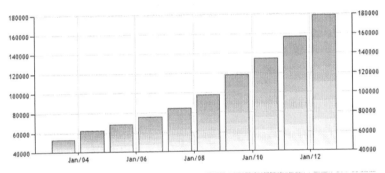

SOURCE: WWW.TRADINGECONOMICS.COM / MINISTRY OF FINANCE, EGYPT

need of Saudi money, employment opportunities for its vast population, and tourist revenues. The struggle against Iran is to be anchored in the needs of both countries. There is Sunni solidarity at work, but more important, cold reasons of statecraft. American influence in the Persian Gulf and the Fertile Crescent is at a low point, a sectarian Sunni-Shia war has wrecked the peace of the region. The Muslim Brotherhood in Cairo and the Saudi rulers know how to bury their differences in order to fight a Shiite enemy.

But the Saudis had no intention of feeding the hand that proposed to bite them. A month later, Saudi Arabia offered Egypt a $235 million loan, a trivial amount indicative of the monarchy's fear and hatred of the Morsi regime.

Already in deep distress, the Egyptian economy began to implode. Basic foodstuffs were no longer within the reach of the poorer half of the population. The price of fava beans, the country's second most important food staple, rose by 40 percent during the spring of 2013, to 5,000 Egyptian pounds per ton from $3,000 Egyptian pounds in January. Imports of proteins collapsed, according to the *Egyptian Gazette*:

> "As for frozen food imports, namely meat, fish and chicken products, they fell by 25 per cent during the first three months of the year, compared to the same period a year before due to the surge in the dollar, "said Alaa Radwan, a member in the Food Stuff Industires at the FECC. Radwan, who is also head of the Association of the Meat, Fish and Chickens Importers, explained that banks had suspended offering importers with letters of credit, demanding them to seek dollars from the parallel market, which caused frozen food prices to increase by 25 per cent to 39 per cent.

The price of imported milk products, which account for 60% to 65% of consumption, rose by 60% since January, the *Gazette* reported. The only basic foodstuffs still available to poor were are state-subsidized bread, sugar and oil, and the bread supply was at risk. The *Financial Times* reported on April 11, 2013 that the Egyptian government would be short 3 to 4 million tons of wheat imports that year. By overestimating the local wheat crop by more than a third, the newspaper quotes an American agricultural attaché, Cairo has slashed orders for imports:

> In a report written by the US agricultural attaché in Cairo, the US warned that the Egyptian government was overestimating production for the current crop year by as much as a third or more. Egypt has predicted it will harvest 9.5m tonnes of wheat this year. The US report put its own estimates 10 per cent lower, at 8.7m tonnes, and warned that several "knowledgeable interlocutors" put the forecast even lower, at 6m–7m tonnes. "The government is setting import procurement and wheat stock policies based on

significant local crop production overestimations," the US agricultural attaché wrote.

Egypt's farmers could not produce that much wheat because they lacked diesel fuel to operate tractors and to bring their harvest to market. The government had just three months' worth of wheat in stockpile and is likely to run short of the country's main foodstuff by earlier summer.

"Egypt has not received a crude oil cargo from open market suppliers since January and, with money tight, the state grain buyer has not purchased wheat since February," Reuters had reported March 28, 2013, adding, "International trading houses Petraco and Arcadia were due to deliver crude after winning a tender, but the state importer, Egyptian General Petroleum Corp (EGPC) has cancelled both deliveries, several traders said. As a result, refineries are running well below capacity."

Not until the military pushed Morsi out of power the following summer did the Gulf States open their checkbooks. The Saudis and the UAE had pledged, but not provided, US$8 billion in loans to Egypt. The moment Morsi was out of power, the *Saudi Gazette* wrote on July 6, 2013:

> Egypt may be able to count on more aid from two other rich Gulf States. Egypt "is in a much better position now to receive aid from Saudi Arabia and the UAE", said Citigroup regional economist Farouk Soussa. "Both Saudi Arabia and the UAE have promised significant financial aid to Egypt. It is more likely that Egypt will receive it now."

It took just two days for the interim government installed last week by Egypt's military to announce that Saudi Arabia and other Gulf States would provide emergency financing for the bankrupt Egyptian state. Egypt may not have a prime minister yet, but it does not really need a prime minister. It has a finance minister, though, and it badly needs a finance minister, especially one with a Rolodex in Riyadh.

As the World Bulletin website reported July 6, 2013:

> "The Finance Ministry has intensified its contacts (with Gulf States) to stand on the volume of financial aid announced,"

caretaker Finance Minister Fayyad Abdel Moneim told the Anadolu Agency in a phone interview Saturday. Abdel Moneim spoke of contacts with Saudi Arabia, the United Arab Emirates (UAE), and Kuwait for urgent aid…Defense Minister Abdel Fatah al-Sisi phoned Saudi Kind Abdullah bin Abdel Aziz and UAE President Sheikh Khalifa bin Zayed al-Nuhayyan yesterday on the latest developments in Egypt. King Abdullah was the first Arab and foreign leader to congratulate interim president Adly Mansour after his swearing-in ceremony.

Meanwhile, Egypt's central bank governor Hisham Ramez was on a plane to Abu Dhabi July 7. The Saudis and the UAE had pledged, but not provided, $8 billion in loans to Egypt, because the Saudi monarchy hates and fears the Muslim Brotherhood as its would-be grave-digger. With the brothers out of power, things might be different. The *Saudi Gazette* wrote July 6:

> Egypt may be able to count on more aid from two other rich Gulf States. Egypt "is in a much better position now to receive aid from Saudi Arabia and the UAE," said Citigroup regional economist Farouk Soussa. "Both Saudi Arabia and the UAE have promised significant financial aid to Egypt. It is more likely that Egypt will receive it now."

Media accounts ignored the big picture, and focused instead on the irrelevant figure of Mohamed al-Baradei, the Nobel Peace Prize winner whose appointment as Prime Minister in the interim government was first announced and then withdrawn on Saturday. It doesn't matter who sits in the Presidential Palace if the country runs out of bread. Tiny Qatar had already expended a third of its foreign exchange reserves during the past year in loans to Egypt, which may explain why the eccentric Emir was replaced in late June by his son. Only Saudi Arabia with its $630 billion of cash reserves has the wherewithal to bridge Egypt's $20 billion a year cash gap. With energy supplies nearly exhausted and just two months' supply of imported wheat on hand, the victor in Cairo will be the Saudi party.

The Saudis had a number of reasons to back the Egyptian military, including the civil war in Syria. Saudi Arabia's intervention in the Syrian civil war, now guided by Prince Bandar, the new chief of Saudi Intelligence, has a double problem. The KSA wants to prevent Iran from turning Syria into a satrapy and fire base, but fears that the Sunni jihadists to whom it is sending anti-aircraft missiles eventually might turn against the monarchy. The same sort of blowback afflicted the kingdom after the 1980s Afghan war, in the person of Osama bin Laden. Saudi Arabia and Qatar have been fighting for influence among Syria's Sunni rebels). The object of cutting off the Muslim Brotherhood at the knees in Egypt was in part to limit the spillover of Islamic radicalism in Syria.

Some Saudi commentators claim al-Sisi as their own, for example Asharq al-Awsat columnist Hussein Shobokshi, who wrote July 7, "God has endowed al-Sisi with the Egyptians' love. In fact, al-Sisi brought a true legitimacy to Egypt, which will open the door to hope after a period of pointlessness, immaturity and distress. Al-Sisi will go down in history and has gained the love of people." The Saudi-funded Salafist (ultra-Islamist) Nour Party in Egypt backed the military coup, probably because it is Saudi-funded, while other Salafists took to the streets with the Muslim Brotherhood to oppose it. Again, none of this matters. The will of a people that cannot feed itself has little weight. Egypt is a banana republic without the bananas.

Since the military expelled Morsi last August, 2,000 members of the Muslim Brotherhood have been arrested, including virtually all of its leadership, and more than 1,000 of its supporters killed in demonstrations.

The Muslim Brotherhood was in no position to resist the Egyptian army, but took out its frustration on Coptic Christians. The Christian Post reported Aug. 15, 2013, "Dozens of churches have been burned down across Egypt over recent weeks, with more than 40 churches said to have come under attack amid widespread unrest in the country. The unrest came to a climax this week when military personnel moved in to quash Muslim Brotherhood protesters who had occupied various regions, calling for attacks and violence against authorities and Christians...As well as more than 40 churches being attacked in recent weeks, homes and businesses of Christians have also been attacked and destroyed by

Islamists. Other attacks also targeted a monastery, three religious societies, three key bookshops belonging to the Bible Society in Egypt, three Christian schools and an orphanage." By October, 85 churches had been destroyed, *Tahrir News* reported Oct. 22, 2013.

Egypt's military responded by offering to rebuild the destroyed churches. "The Egyptian defense minister ordered the engineering department of the armed forces to swiftly repair all the affected churches, in recognition of the historical and national role played by our Coptic brothers," according to a government statement read on Egyptian television Aug. 20.

The military government, to be sure, continues to rule with a heavy hand, suppressing Muslim Brotherhood holdouts in ways that offend Western sensibilities. In November 2013 an Alexandria court sentenced young female activists for the Brotherhood to eleven years in prison for violating bans on demonstrations, prompting further protests in the final days of the month. Human Rights Watch December 1 called on the military government to release five aides of former President Morsi still in detention.

Egypt survives today on artificial life support, thanks to more than $15 billion of emergency aid from Saudi Arabia and other Gulf States, despite drastic cuts in American aid. Egypt's military led by key figures from the Mubarak era is back in control. In contrast to the grim summer of 2013, when food and energy supplies nearly ran out, Egyptians had access to basic necessities at the close of the year.

The Muslim Brotherhood has been outlawed and decapitated by the restored military regime. The jihadist Sheikh Qaradawi continues to call for its violent overthrow, denouncing Defense Minister al-Sisi as a "traitor." As the Saudi English-language web newspaper *Asharq al-Awsat* warned Nov. 25, 2013:

The July 3 military action that deposed Mursi and killed many of his supporters shocked Qaradawi. His reaction reflected his anger and disappointment in the reversal of the Muslim Brotherhood's fortunes. Several days after Mursi was removed, Qaradawi issued a fatwa saying, "It is haram [religiously impermissible] for Egypt to do this.... Nothing can come after this except divine wrath and punishment."

Subsequently, he issued another fatwa calling on "Muslims from around the world" to be shuhada, or martyrs, in Egypt, adding: "Allah will ask you on the day of judgment whether you saw these human massacres."

Qaradawi's reaction to the August 14 military crackdown on the Muslim Brotherhood occupation of Rabaa Al-Adawiya Square was even more pointed. Nearly one thousand Brotherhood supporters were killed during the clearing of the square, as the military and the pro-Mursi camp clashed. That day, Qaradawi made a lengthy speech on Al-Jazeera's Egyptian channel encouraging all Egyptians to "go out to the streets" and confront the military. Qaradawi described this as a "fardi ayn" (religious duty), an "obligation for every able-bodied and believing Egyptian to leave their house." Minister of Defense Abdel-Fattah El-Sisi and the Egyptian government were "complicit in these massacres," Qaradawi added, and would "have to answer to Allah for what they have done."

It is a sign of the times that the commentary in this semi-official Saudi site was written by the American analyst David Schenker, a former aide to Secretary of Defense Donald Rumsfeld. Schenker added that al-Sisi's government has been cracking down on jihadists in the Sinai and Gaza:

> In recent months, the Egyptian military has been taking steps to shore up the border with Gaza in order to prevent the infiltration of weapons, Hamas members, and foreign fighters aligned with Al-Qaeda into Egypt's increasingly dangerous Sinai Peninsula. ..Some one hundred members of the security forces have been killed in recent months in the Sinai. Meanwhile, Egypt's Muslim Brotherhood—and, seemingly, Qaradawi—oppose the efforts to reestablish security in the peninsula, hoping to leverage the ongoing violence for political concessions to the Islamists.

The problem, of course, is that Egypt's insecurity is not limited to the Sinai. Since Mursi's removal this summer, terrorists have targeted a state-owned satellite television station in a Cairo suburb with rocket-propelled grenades and attempted to assassinate the interior minister with a car bomb in downtown Cairo. Equally problematic Sinai-based insurgents fired rockets at a ship traversing the Suez Canal in late August.

Israel is at worst a bystander and at best a de facto ally of the Saudis. The Saudi Wahabbists hate Israel, to be sure, and would be happy if the Jewish State and all its inhabitants vanished tomorrow. But Israel presents no threat at all to Riyadh, while Iran represents an existential threat. The Saudis, we know from Wikileaks, begged the United States to attack Iran, or to let Israel do so.

Strategic Consequences

The ending to the story of the Egyptian Spring might be not be happy, but it may be salutary in one important way. When the Muslim Brotherhood came to power with the blessing of the Obama administration and the ideological sympathy of mainstream Republicans, Egypt and the Middle East looked into an abyss of hunger and chaos. The Egyptian people stepped back from the abyss and chose the temporary stability of military rule over the opium-dream of Islamic democracy, and the wealthy Gulf States intervened to prevent economic disaster. Israel, Egypt and Saudi Arabia all understand that they have a common interest in preventing jihadists from gaining control of major governments. The Egyptian experience has helped the Sunni Arab world gain clarity about its challenges and interests. It has demonstrated to a number of important Arab governments, including the Saudis, that Israel is the least of their enemies, and that nemesis is likeliest to appear from within. There may be a chance to establish regional stability in the absence of the United States.

For the Egyptian people, the resolution of the crisis has gained critical time. Sadly, Egypt cannot survive without a subsidy far more generous than the West is willing to provide. The crisis has persuaded the Gulf States to help Egypt on a scale hitherto unforeseen, and that gives Egypt economic breathing room. From the standpoint of development economics, Egypt is an intractable case. When people are hungry, though, it is always preferable to eat now and deal with fundamental problems later.

Russia is certainly a winner in the Egyptian outcome, but it is not clear to what extent its gains will alter the strategic balance in the Eastern Mediterranean. Egypt has demonstrated that it has alternative sources of weapons and financing than the United States, and that American attempts to mold Egyptian politics to fit the ideological preferences of either party are unlikely to succeed. Apart from a few billion dollars' worth of arms sales, though, Russia can achieve little in Egypt. It does not share the burden of supporting a regime crippled by long-term economic crisis. Rumors have circulated of a much deeper Russian-Egyptian military understanding, for example, a Russian naval base in Alexandria. But Russia's forces in the Eastern Mediterranean are meagre compared to the Soviet-era navy and it is not at all clear that Russia would do with a local base. Ruslan Aliev of the Moscow Center for Analysis of Strategies and Technologies told Defense News Nov. 24, 2013: "Since the Soviet Union, the naval deployment has been on the sea. [The Syrian port of] Tartus is not a [Russian] base. It only provides a small technical hub. So a naval base in Alexandria is not in line with Russian naval operations in the Mediterranean."

The depth of Egypt's crisis is a gauge of its own diminishing importance: the largest Arab country has become the sick man of North Africa, dependent on an enormous subsidy and in continuous danger of regressing into political instability. It is failing as a nation, incapable of sustaining itself or of inflicting much harm on its neighbors. There is of course a risk that Egypt's economic crisis might give rise to political adventures: a grab for Libyan oil, for example, or Ethiopian water. A longer-range risk is that the deterioration of the Egyptian state will turn the country into a Petrie dish for Islamic terrorists.

The effects of an Egypt state failure might include:

I. **The departure of large numbers of economic refugees for southern Europe**

The civil wars in Libya and Syria provoked "one of the largest movements of migrants across the Mediterranean, with numbers accelerating fast," the London Guardian reported Oct. 13, 2013. The United Nations High Commission on Refugees reports,

"More than 4,600 left Libya in September, compared to 755 in the same month last year. Of the 32,000 who have landed in Italy this year so far, 7,500 are Syrian and a further 7,500 Eritrean." Libya has been the main source of refugees. With only 6 million people, Libya already presents a humanitarian crisis. According to UNHCR, 656,000 people, mostly migrant workers from Egypt and Tunisia, had fled Libya's civil war during 2011. Although the volume of refugees has slowed since 2011, it remains at critical levels. Egypt has 80 million people, and a breakdown of civil society in the most populous Arab country would likely give rise to a humanitarian disaster an order of magnitude greater than the problem of 2013. European naval and humanitarian resources already are overstretched, and would be swamped by a refugee influx from Egypt.

II. Destabilization of Egypt's border with Libya

In the event of extreme need, oil-poor Egypt might attempt to take over Libya's substantial oil reserves. Chaos inside Libya might provide the pretext for intervention. In January 2014, Egypt detained the chief of a Libyan militia, Shaaban Hadia-al-Zway. Immediately afterwards five members of the Egyptian embassy staff in Tripoli were kidnapped by Libyan militias. In an apparent prisoner exchange, al-Zway and the kidnapped Egyptian diplomats both were released.

III. The acquisition of sophisticated Egyptian armed forces weapons by terrorists in Gaza or the Sinai

Egypt's armed forces so far have maintained their cohesion against the Islamist opposition. If Egypt's military failed to suppress the Muslim Brotherhood and civil conflict were prolonged, discipline in the Egyptian military could not be guaranteed and defections from the military to the Islamists would be a likely outcome. Egypt's insurgent Islamists have already downed army aircraft with sophisticated man-portable air defense systems (MANPADS).

According to IHS-Janes, the shoulder-fired rocket that Islamists used to shoot down an Egyptian military helicopter on Jan. 25, 2014 was a sophisticated Igla-type (SA-18) Russian or Chinese system obtained either from the dispersed Libyan stockpile or from Iran. The Egyptian military currently possesses more than 600 Igla-type MANPADS and more than 1,800 Stingers. If these and other sophisticated weapons leaked out to Islamists the scale of the conflict in Egypt would escalate, perhaps to Syrian proportions. The danger to civil as well as military aviation would be profound.

IV. Closure of the Suez Canal

Islamist terrorists have already taken credit for rocket-propelled grenade attacks on ships passing through the Suez Canal. In September 2013, a group calling itself the al-Furqan Brigades posted a Youtube video claiming to show an RPG attack on a container ship. If Islamists obtained more powerful weapons, for example any of the wire-guided anti-tank missiles in the Egyptian Army's arsenal, the threat to Suez Canal shipping would become serious.

V. Agitation among the more than two million Egyptian foreign workers in Jordan and the Gulf States.

The Gulf monarchies depend extensively on guest workers, who form a majority of some of the smaller states. Most of the 8 million inhabitants of the United Arab Emirates are foreign workers. Security officials of the Gulf States have accused the Muslim Brotherhood of plotting their overthrow. Dubai's Chief of Police Dahi Khalfan claimed in July 2012: "There's an international plot against Gulf states in particular and Arab countries in general... This is pre-planned to take over our fortunes. The bigger our sovereign wealth funds and the more money we put in the banks of Western countries, the bigger the plot to take over our countries... The Brothers and their governments in Damascus and North Africa have to know that the Gulf is a red line, not only for Iran but also for the Brothers as well." Civil disorder in Egypt might find resonance among Egyptian and other foreign workers in the Gulf and create security problems there.

America's best option is to work with the Saudis and the Egyptian military to reduce the likelihood that any of these risks might be realized. In the short term there is no alternative to Gulf State financial support to keep the lights on and the bakeries open. Restoration of order might bring some amelioration by restoring Egypt's tourist industry, which earned only $5.9 billion in 2013, about half the $11 billion earned in 2008. In the medium term, Egypt requires extensive investment in infrastructure, agriculture and manufacturing to reverse six decades of economic mismanagement. The United States and Europe are poorly positioned to undertake such investments, which involve high risk and a slow payout of returns. It is more likely that China will step in to the void that is now the Egyptian economy. As the dominant investor in Africa, China has a long-term interest in transportation and telecommunications links between the Eurasian continent and Africa, for which Egypt is a natural bridge.

The cumulative errors in American foreign policy—long-term support for an ineffective and corrupt military government, the sudden abandonment of Hosni Mubarak, and the flirtation with the Muslim Brotherhood—may lead to a vacuum of influence in Egypt which China eventually may fill, erasing the effect of decades of American diplomacy and investment.

(Note: some of this material was previously published
by the author in Asia Times *and* The Tablet.*)*

Epilogue

IN OUR OPENING SECTIONS, we recognized that as we examined each country under a strategic/economic security criterion, we would have to include time as an independent variable because the passage of time is almost always a deciding factor in the history of nations.

We know, for example, that the Egyptian military government headed by General al-Sisi believes it can last out the current US administration in hopes of gaining greater and more consistent support from another administration. The increasingly severe food shortages suffered by the Egyptian people could prove al-Sisi wrong by making his nation a fertile area for an insurgency, possibly including the Muslim Brotherhood, to topple his government.

How will Turkey's Erdogan survive his nation's economic crises? It may be that his regime has had such success in turning Turkey's military away from its role as the protector of the nation's secularism. Whether or not Erdogan has succeeded in reaching that goal, it appears that without assistance his government will be replaced in the next few years by a military coup or an election.

The Saudi royal family, though it appears stable in the near term, is highly susceptible to Iran's action in the eastern provinces. Those actions, which we have discussed, are far more likely to occur than not and though they will likely be sufficient to destabilize the nation, they may not be sufficient to topple the Saudi government. Nevertheless, when Iran achieves its nuclear weapons ambitions, a Saudi Arabia—cut loose from American foreign policy as it is now and seeking its own nuclear arsenal—may destabilize itself.

We believe that these brief studies will be of considerable value to America's and other nations' policymakers in determining the how these three nations will prosper, endure, or simply fail in the next three to five years. These studies, we believe, prove the concept with which we began: that some unexpected events in foreign policy can be made more predictable by the application of our criteria. We hope and expect that, as we continue these studies, the concept will become more widely known and generally accepted in the policymaking community.

—Herb London, Jed Babbin and David Goldman.

Made in the USA
Lexington, KY
03 January 2015